FIELD ARCHERY

FIELD ARCHERY

DON STAMP

ADAM & CHARLES BLACK

LONDON

FIRST PUBLISHED 1979

BY A AND C BLACK (PUBLISHERS) LTD.

35 BEDFORD ROW, LONDON WC1R 4JH

© 1979 DON STAMP

ISBN 0 7136 1981 3

Stamp, Don
  Field Archery.
  1. Archery
I. Title
799.3'2   GV1185
ISBN 0–7136–1981–3

Printed and bound in Great Britain
at The Pitman Press, Bath

To all those who have shared with me

the fascination of Field.

CONTENTS

ILLUSTRATIONS

Plates

Figures

FOREWORD

When I wrote *The Challenge of Archery* eight years ago there was a need for a practical manual in which archers of all grades of ability and experience could find useful advice. In that book field archery quite properly found its place, but owing to the scope of the work could not be treated in depth. Since that time, field archery has developed very rapidly and I have become more and more involved in it. I would claim that my interest and activity embraces the whole of archery, but it is true that my chief personal pleasure in actually shooting comes from practising field. I hope that I have communicated some of that pleasure in this book, along with such practical advice as I can muster. Its purpose is to bring more recruits and converts to field archery – that is why it progresses from the most elementary principles to the more advanced, and why it considers field archery in its wider aspects.

I would like to acknowledge my indebtedness to my wife, Fionna, who is as deeply involved in field as I am. Every day we discuss field archery and the form in which these ideas are expressed is very much a combined effort. My thanks, too, to my son Robert who posed for and assisted with the instructional photographs, and to all those archers without whose companionship and zest for constructive argument this book would not have been written.

Don Stamp

METRIC CONVERSION

At the time of writing, both metric and imperial measurements are in current use, and where practicable both measurements have been given. The following tables may also be found useful.

Length

1 inch	=	0.0254 metre		
1 foot	=	0.3048		
1 yard	=	0.9144		
1 metre	=	1 yard	0 feet	3.37 inches
5 metres	=	5	1	4.85
10	=	10	2	9.70
30	=	32	2	5.10
50	=	54	2	0.50
60	=	65	1	10.20

Weight

1 grain	=	0.065 grams
1 pound	=	0.45359 kilograms
1 gram	=	15.4 grains
1 kilogram	=	2.20462 lbs

Area

1 acre	=	0.40469 hectares
1 hectare	=	2.47105 acres

1

WHAT IS FIELD ARCHERY?

A great deal of variety is possible in archery, yet basically all the different forms have one major thing in common and that is to hit the mark you are aiming at. There is not much satisfaction unless you can do this fairly often and, of course, improving your skill in this respect is what archery is all about. Hitting the mark is the essential point of target archery, clout, popinjay, rovers, and adaptations of other games, like archery golf and archery darts. It is not the point of flight shooting (for sheer distance) or of archery in Zen (where it is part of a mental and spiritual discipline). But these other archery pursuits each have their own special justification.

Another objective common to all archery today is 'doing it the hard way' – namely, by use of the bow in preference to a rifle, by the exercise of one's own physical strength, steadiness and skill. The degree to which extra aids are employed, such as sights, stabilisers, levelling devices, mechanical systems, and so on, is a matter of personal preference, but their use is controlled by the laws of the sport when competitive shooting is undertaken.

But how does field archery differ from these other varieties? (Paradoxically, part of the answer is that whereas target archery takes place on a flat field, field archery is practised preferably in woods and on slopes and not usually on a field.)

Target archers shoot stated numbers of arrows from a few set distances within one competitive round; for example, York round: 6 dozen arrows at 100 yards, 4 dozen at 80 yards and 2 dozen at 60 yards. In the course then, of a day's shooting over the York round, the target archer will shoot at only three distances, all measured and checked for accuracy, all in the same direction, and at a speed regulated by the rules, taking no longer than 2½ minutes to loose three arrows. All archers will move forward together to collect arrows and to record scores, and resume shooting together under the control of a 'field captain,' or 'judge', with a whistle. The targets will be the same size at all distances and marked in concentric rings, and everyone will know what size they are. Probably all archers will use sights, and most archers will use more sophisticated aids as allowed for under the rules. They will sit down and rest between spells of shooting, or may retire into their own personal tents if the weather is bad. At important meetings they will be informed of the leading scores throughout the tournament by a leader-board rather like a cricket score-board. Target archery is a fine sport, demanding discipline and concentration of a high order, and in spite of the impression that might be gained from the above description, demanding strength, fitness and endurance, both mental and physical; it provides a great challenge to those who practise it.

Field archery, on the other hand, involves spending a day on the move, round a course of a size limited only by the necessity of providing, say, 14 or 28 targets in safety – it could be 4 acres (1.6 hectares) or it could be 40. The distances at which the targets will be placed will vary considerably. Even on the Standard FITA (Fédération Internationale de Tir à l'Arc) Field round where distances are marked, there will be targets set at 14 distances from 6 metres to 60 metres, and no more than four arrows will ever be shot consecutively at the same distance. On the other hand, if a FITA Hunter round is shot, the distances from which the shots will be taken will not be marked at all and have to be estimated by judgement alone, and not by any form of measuring aid. There will never be more than one shot from each post, and the distances can be at any irregular measurement within the limits permitted according to the size of the target. For example, a 60 cm target might be shot at 46.5 metres, 39 metres, 37.5 and 31 metres, one arrow from each post. In this round no binoculars may be used, as target archers are allowed.

Again, the size of the faces varies, from 15 cm to 60 cm in the FITA rounds; the colours vary according to the type of round, and so do the scoring values. If an 'animal' round is shot, then there will be naturalistic faces either in colour or monochrome. Scoring may depend on whether a hit is scored on 1st, 2nd or 3rd shot, and on whether the animal is 'killed' or 'wounded'. Even total silhouettes may be shot at, animals and birds portrayed in their natural sizes in their natural colours, as in the British Wild Life round – bringing field archery very near to bow-hunting, but without the arguable charge of cruelty often brought against the latter sport.

These shots may be set on uphill or downhill slopes of varying degrees of severity, into or out of the light, across lakes or gullies, from difficult standing positions, or in the face of twigs, leaves or brush or natural hazards. Some shots could be set on open wind-swept terrain; others in dense 'jungle'. So you can see that during a day's shooting over a 30 acre (12 hect) course, an archer gets a good deal of exercise, mental and physical, in shooting, say, 112 arrows. The target archer will have shot his arrows with care and deliberation in conditions which are made as uniform as possible; the field archer will have used care and deliberation too, but in situations that vary from shot to shot throughout the day. This is, in fact, the fascination of field – its greater variety compared with target archery. There is no conflict between target and field; an increasing number of archers practise both, but the disciplines of each have a different appeal and emphasis.

So far I have not said anything about styles of shooting. Some field archers, freestylers, use very similar equipment and methods to those used by target archers, but a very numerous class of field archers prefer to shoot barebow, ie without sights, or any of the other aids that a freestyler has to help him (and, it must be admitted, has to learn to control). Some use, by choice, wooden arrows instead of alloy or fibreglass shafts, such wooden arrows often being made at home with great skill and care. The ultra-traditionalists use longbows of the same design as those which won the battles of Crécy, Poitiers and Agincourt. At the other end of the scale, there is an increasing following of those who wish to use compound bows, incorporating a mechanical advantage by use of pulleys to provide greater power with less apparent effort, with or without release aids, sights or other attachments.

From the descriptions of preferred terrain, types of target and styles of shooting, it might appear that field archery is merely a watered-down form of bow-hunting. It is true that field archery originated in America as a means whereby bow-hunters might keep in practice during the close season for hunting game, by using their normal equipment, only replacing the lethal broad-heads by blunt piles of the same weight, but from that beginning field archery has developed into a sport in its own right – it is in fact a very modern development of the ancient skill of archery. In the following pages I hope to deal with those aspects of the sport which will enable anyone, whether he is already an archer or a complete beginner, to share with me the fascination of field.

2

MAKING A START

Once you have decided which style you wish to shoot – for simplicity's sake this can be reduced to freestyle or barebow – you will then require equipment to use while you are learning. Of course, it may be that you have not decided which style to use and wish to try both. No matter – you can learn on the same equipment.

You would be well advised to join a specialist field archery club or one which takes an interest in field archery as well as target archery. There are a number of reasons for this:

1   It will provide suitable ground and facilities for you to learn on.
2   It may very well have a pool of equipment for you as a beginner to use at a small charge.
3   It will have someone trained to coach, or at any rate members with experience who will be only too pleased to assist the beginner.
4   It will provide the companionship that is an essential part of archery.
5   You will be in touch with the mainspring of archery and absorb all sorts of stimulating ideas that would never occur to you on your own.
6   You will also be covered for third party insurance while under instruction, and later if you join as a full member.

All this need not be at all expensive, for clubs are generally eager to recruit new members, and quite expect to have to teach complete novices and make them welcome. Beginners' fees are low by any standard and members' fees in archery are really quite modest compared with those entailed in other sports. But it may be that for various reasons you are either obliged to start on your own or wish to do so, in which case the following systems of training can be followed.

First you must have somewhere to shoot that is safe. Bearing in mind that an arrow from even a light practice bow may travel at 150 feet (46m) per second, that a blunt-nosed arrow can penetrate corrugated iron quite easily and that a simple training bow of, say, 32 lbs (14.5 kg) draw-weight can send an arrow at least 180 yards, it is obvious that a back-garden is not at all suitable unless maybe it is bordered by open fields which no passers-by can enter undetected. It is better to look for a piece of ground that you can have permission to use away from public access, and preferably covered with short grass or some other surface that will not hide those arrows that miss the target. If the ground provides some sort of natural back-stop like a bank of turf or sand, so much the better. For field archery it need not be particularly flat, though I would not advise steep slopes at this stage. You must never shoot towards areas where people or animals may stray, especially if they cannot be seen by you when they do so.

Now you need something to shoot at, something that will act as a butt and stop the arrows. Orthodox butts of coiled straw rope or tightly compressed straw board can be purchased, but they are an unnecessary outlay for the beginner. Bales of straw or hay are not too difficult to come by, but will need to be firmly lashed together if arrows are not to penetrate between the bales. Cheapest of all is the corrugated cardboard from flattened down boxes that once held refrigerators or TV sets, for example. Fold these down, take out any metal staples or metal strips, and lash together with strong string about 16 to 20 thicknesses of the material. This will easily stop arrows from the sort of bow you will begin by using. I recommend that you make a rectangular butt about 4' by 3' (about a metre square). Provide yourself with four pieces of wood, roughly 5' long (1.5m) and 1" by 2" (25 x 50mm) in thickness and point the ends so that they can be driven into the ground with a mallet.

Now that you have somewhere to shoot and something to shoot at, you will need some tackle to shoot with. First you will have to decide whether you are going to shoot right-handed or left-handed and you cannot always decide for yourself without actually trying it. Most people, you see, have a dominant eye – a tendency to use one eye in preference to the other for the purpose of aiming. It is very likely that it is the stronger eye, but it might not be. This eye should be the one behind the arrow as you aim and shoot; that is to say, the eye furthest from the target. This means that if you are right-eyed and right-handed there is no problem. You hold the bow in the left hand and aim with the right eye. Likewise the left-eyed archer who is left-handed has no problem. He holds the bow in his right hand and aims with the left eye.

But what of the person who is left-handed and right-eye dominant or vice versa? Well, he can close the dominant eye and hold the bow as seems natural. If he can still see to aim with the non-dominant eye, it could be a satisfactory solution, but he would be limited in watching the fall of the arrows, which can be better observed with binocular vision (ie with both eyes open). Alternatively he could use the dominant eye (that is, with both eyes open) and change hands. At first this will seem awkward, but it will soon pass away.

To test yourself to find out which eye is dominant, the following procedure is usually informative. Get a cardboard tube about 8″ (20cm) long such as is used for the core of kitchen paper rolls. Keeping *both* eyes open, (this is important) hold the tube at arm's length in such a way as to look through it at some small object, say a clock face or a door handle across the width of a room. Now, keeping the 'aim' on the object, move the tube back until it covers one of your eyes. That will be your dominant eye, the one you aim with. You see, you *have* just aimed with it along the tube. If you get no positive result , or varying results, it could be that you have no preferred eye, and use either indiscriminately. In this case, you may shoot as suits your right- or left-handedness, but close the eye on the bow-hand side while aiming, until such time as you have got used to picking up the aim with the eye on the string-hand side. Ideally then, the right-eyed archer holds the bow in the left hand, draws the string with the right hand and aims with the right eye, even though both eyes may be open. The left-eyed archer ideally holds the bow in the right hand, draws the string with the left hand and aims with the left eye even when both eyes are open.

On the question of tackle, while it is possible to make almost everything an archer uses if you have the materials, the tools and the skill, no-one inexperienced in archery could do this, so such equipment must either be bought or borrowed. Borrowing I don't recommend – the equipment might not be suitable for you, and where does it leave you if any of it breaks while you are using it? (I am excluding the borrowing of club equipment used under the supervision of a qualified coach, of course.)

So that means purchase. It may be that your local general sports dealer stocks some archery tackle, but this is usually suitable for the casual market of children and youths who treat bows and arrows as toys (very unwisely, I might add). So unless you have a companion archer who can go with you to see what can be provided locally you would be well advised to deal with one of the specialist archery suppliers, all of whom have a mail order business, and some of whom provide credit facilities. Whether you are able to call at the store or peruse the catalogue, you will be amazed at the sophistication of the equipment offered, and some of the top prices may stagger you, because, let's face it, top quality goods, the products of skill and expensive processing are liable to be costly. But what you need to start archery is relatively cheap.

At this point you might be tempted to lash out and spend far more than you had originally intended in order to buy 'something that will last'. Well, don't! If you buy a tournament bow of 45 lb (20 kg) draw-weight you won't be able to handle it, because you won't yet have the technique. If you buy an expensive bow that is easy to handle to start with, you will soon become dissatisfied with it and want a more powerful model. Your arrows may prove not to be the right length after you've used them a while, and you will realise that you are likely to lose or damage some of your first set of arrows through inexperience, no matter how careful you may be. No, I suggest you get a solid fibre-glass bow of about 32 lbs (14.5 kg) @ 28″ (71 cm) if you are a man, and about 26 lbs (12 kg) @ 28″ if you are a lady.

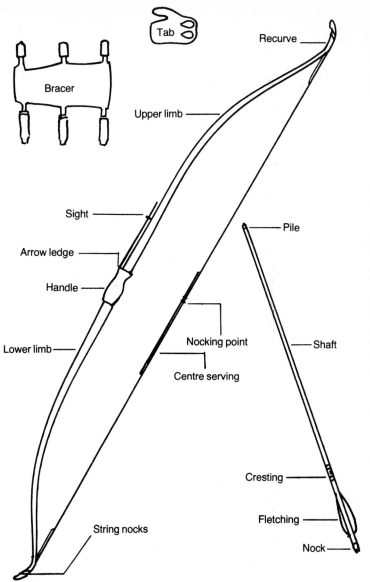

FIGURE 1   Beginner's equipment

Children below 14 years old might have smaller bows com-
mensurate with their size and strength. These are to learn on.
When you no longer need them, you can pass them on or sell

them second-hand, for they are virtually indestructible and maintain their shooting powers indefinitely. Whether you get a straight-ended bow or one with a slight recurve is not important, but those with a recurve do have a slightly better performance. All these bows may be shot right or left-handed.

Next, arrows. These must be long enough to be drawn in safety by the beginner, which means they should be longer than those he will eventually use. A good quick test is to place the nock of the arrow on the top of the breast-bone and stretch out both hands towards the pile of the arrow, as far as you can reach.

This distance from the chest to the tips of the middle fingers represents the length of arrow you will probably be able to draw. A beginner is advised to use arrows that are 1″ or 2″ longer, so that he cannot draw the arrow inside the bow or onto his hand. It may be that by this test a man 6′ tall will find that he requires a training arrow of 29″ or 30″. All right, that's safe. They can be shortened quite easily later on if necessary, when you settle to an even draw-length. But what about the bow which is marked at 28″, you may ask. Is there risk of damage to it, if this distance is exceeded? Well, no, not with a solid fibre-glass bow – with a laminated tournament bow, yes, one would need to consider the stated draw-length, but even here the manufacturers will state what the maximum draw-length should be, and a certain amount of over-draw is allowed for. With the solid fibre-glass bow there is no need to bother about an inch or two. Arrows are sold usually in sets of 8. Get an inexpensive set of a length that suits you, and of stiffness, or 'spine', that suits the bow you are going to use. Alloy shafts will be best at this stage even if you anticipate using wooden ones later on in Traditional Class, because they are more durable. They should be fitted with feather fletching as they then can be shot off the ledge on the bow-handle. If plastic fletching is used you will have to purchase an arrow-rest to stick on the bow, and this rest must be either right or left-handed.

Two more items of equipment and we have done. First a bracer; this is worn on the inside of the bow-arm to keep loose clothing out of the way and to provide some protection against a careless loose. There is a great variety of these provided by the suppliers – all you need is one that fits comfortably and is secured by two or three straps. It need not be expensive. Lastly, the tab. This must fit exactly so that it just covers the shooting fingers, and so that the finger-holes are neither too tight nor too loose. It may need trimming a little. The tab should be of a simple two-hole design to fit over the two middle fingers. The material of which it is made should be either leather or a man-made substitute. Make sure it fits the hand which is to draw the string, for tabs are made either right or left-handed; they are not reversible.

To start archery you do not need any other equipment. Such useful articles as quivers are best left until you find out what design you prefer. You might, however, buy 4 paper Standard round faces with black and white roundels, and 4 Hunter round faces with white centre spot, to put on your target butt. These should be 15 cm, 30 cm, 45 cm and 60 cm; (or 6″, 1′, 18″ and 2′ sizes).

Now you must prepare your bow for use. The nocking point must be put on the string. Brace the bow as the instructions suggest or as you have been shown in the shop. Make sure you have bent it the right way round. Find the point on the string which is at right-angles to the arrow-ledge, or rest if you are using one. You can do this by using a set-square or a corner of cut paper. Now mark the string 3 mm above this point. Try an arrow on the string. It should clip on lightly, so that it will stay on the string until the string is tapped smartly, whereupon it should fall off. If it is too loose, thicken the centre-serving at this point with an extra binding of thread, or better, of dental floss if you can get it. When the nocking point has been built up to the right thickness, you can whip a small binding above and below the nocking-point to prevent the arrow slipping up and down.

If you are going to shoot freestyle you will need something to serve as a sight. Stick a 15 cm strip of draught-stopping foam or medical plaster down the back of the bow just above the handle, that is to say, on the side of the bow that has the outside curve. In this, stick a glass-headed pin or something similar to serve as a simple sight.

3

BASIC METHODS

FREESTYLE

Clothing should be suitable for the season and comfortable, but the upper garment should be close-fitting. Low-heeled shoes are best. Make sure you have no ornaments, metal badges, or pens in pockets that could be caught by the bow-string. Choose the piece of ground you are to use by selecting an area reasonably free from growth that could conceal arrows, and elect to shoot in a direction away from the sun. See that there are no people or animals around that could be endangered. Set up your target butt by driving the four stakes into the ground and sandwiching the butt between them, as seen incidentally in Plate 3. Tie the tops of the stakes together firmly to keep everything secure. Fix the largest field face, the 60 cm one, in the middle of the butt by using sticky tape on the corners. Don't use nails lest an arrow strike them and get blunted. Failing a field face, you could use anything as an aiming mark – a beer mat, for instance.

Now retire about 15 metres, put in a foot-marker or post and brace your bow as instructed. The following directions are those for a right-hander. Left-handed archers (or those shooting left-handed) should make the necessary modifications. Set the sight pin as far above the arrow-ledge as your eye is above your chin. You can use your thumb and forefinger like a pair of callipers to feel the measurement on your face before transferring it to the bow. Put the pin on the left-hand side of the bow limb (right-hand side for left-handers). The head should project only about 3 mm. Rest the bow on some convenient support. It is advisable not to lay it directly on the ground. Take out 4 arrows from the box and put them by the bow. Fasten the bracer on the inside of

FIGURE 2   Shoulder line

the left fore-arm, and slip the tab onto the correct fingers of the right hand.

Stand sideways to the target with the left shoulder towards it, the feet a comfortable distance astride, left toe to the post. Without looking at the target, raise both arms sideways to shoulder height. Keeping the shoulders square, turn the head and observe the target over the left hand. It is of no particular importance where the feet are placed, because in an actual field shoot, the standing positions will be dictated by the terrain. What is of the utmost importance is to see that the line through the shoulders is direct to the target. For the moment, as long as you are standing in a well-balanced, comfortable position that allows you to adopt the correct shoulder position, that is satisfactory. At this point you can test flexibility at the hips by swivelling your torso gently from the hips to see how much rotation you can make of the shoulders without moving the feet. Now try gently rocking from side to side at the hips, so that the shoulder line is tilted up and down as shown in Figure 2. This sort of flexibility is essential for field archers, much more than for target archers, because field targets are often sited on slopes and diagonally across slopes.

Now drop the arms and walk away from the place where you were standing before returning to set up your standing position again, seeing that your bow and arrows are within easy reach. Next, the head turn. Imagine your head is like an orange on a stick. Look level, your own height, straight in front of you, and then gently turn your head towards the target, preserving the upright posture, until you can just clearly see all of the target across the bridge of your nose even when your left eye is closed to check. You should not need to turn your head more than this, unless you wear glasses, in which case you might have to turn a little further to get a clear image.

Now take the bow by the left hand at the handle and hold it in a naturally closed hold with the string against the inside of the left arm. Do not grip it tightly. Make sure that your hand does not project above the handle, for the arrow must lie on the ledge, not on your hand. To check that you are holding it correctly, place the thumb up the inside of the bow and then close it round naturally. If this is done properly, the bow-string will be seen to be clear of the bracer. If the string touches the bracer, the wrist is too much turned into the bow, and the hold should be adjusted.

Without using the right hand at all, present the bow held vertically at arm's length to the target, keeping your shoulders squarely lined to the target as in the first exercise. Keeping the left elbow high, bring the bow hand and the bow to touch the left shoulder by bending at the elbow. Straighten the elbow again and restore the bow to its position at arm's length. You will see that the crease in the elbow joint is now vertical and not horizontal. It must be vertical so that the elbow does not come into the way of the string. As long as the elbow is set sideways, the arm can be quite straight in a strong position. Some people have very flexible joints, but you should not allow the arm to lock back on itself, but let it remain straight with the elbow sideways. This is important. Of course, one does not go through this performance every time before shooting; this is an exercise for the beginner. The correct position will soon become second nature.

Without an arrow, place the first three fingers of the right hand on the bow-string, one finger above the nocking point and the other two below it, with a small space between first and second finger – where, in fact, the slot of the tab is. The tab should be between your fingers and the string, but you should be able to feel the string locating in the groove of the end joint. Keep the hand flat and the fingers flat, only lightly hooking the terminal joint to secure the string. Keep the thumb back away from the string. Hold the bow in a diagonal position slightly towards the target. Do not move the shoulders but turn the head to the required position to see the target properly across the bridge of the nose. In a moment you are going to draw the bow as if to shoot, but you are not to let go of the string. It would not harm this solid fibre-glass bow to loose without an arrow, but it could shatter a more expensive laminated bow, so don't do it at all. If you feel insecure in that you might let the string slip off the tab by accident, then flap it back and put your bare fingers on the string. It won't hurt, for you aren't going to shoot yet.

By using the shoulders and upper arms in unison draw the

bow fully, at the same time bringing it to the vertical towards the target. Locate the string hand under the chin which should be kept level, and draw the string to contact middle of chin, middle of lips and middle of nose. Don't poke your chin at it. Once you have established this, 'come down', that is to say, take the power off the bow without letting go of the string, and come back to the starting position and rest. Do this as many times as is necessary for you to come to the position on the face, the anchor-point as it is called, without too much fumbling.

Next, aiming. If you have any reason to suppose that you may have difficulty in picking up the sight with the correct eye, which for you as a right-hander is the right eye, you could close the left eye before starting this exercise. Draw full, anchor firmly, distribute the draw-weight of the bow across the shoulders evenly and see where the sight is. If it is not in the middle of the target, swivel or tilt from the hips to bring it there, hold it on aim for a few seconds, then relax and come down without loosing the string. Do not move the arms alone to achieve this aim; do it by movement of the whole of the upper part of the body.

This has been a necessary exercise in handling the bow. Now we must bring the arrow into the picture. Pick up an arrow by the cresting, thumb in front of the cock feather (the one at right-angles to the slot of the nock) and lay the shaft over the bow, across the arrow-ledge and push the nock onto the string at the nocking point, where it should stay secure and snug. The cock feather will thus not be able to contact the bow while it is being shot – this is as it should be.

Place the fingers, with or without the tab, on the string, one finger above the nock and two below it. Let the forefinger just lightly touch the nock, but make sure that the second finger is clear of it by at least 3 mm. Flatten the fingers and the hand, and line up the hand and the fore-arm in a straight line with the arrow shaft as in Plate 1. Without raising the bow, draw back the string with the arrow on it about a foot or so, not very far. Hold it still for a moment and then loose the arrow into the ground, by letting the string slide off the fingers. Do this a good many times, the object of the exercise being not merely to familiarise yourself with the feel of the loose, but more particularly to get the draw –

stop – aim – pause – loose routine established, and to ensure that both bow arm and string arm are playing equal part in the performance. If the loose is done properly, both hands will move apart a little as the arrow is shot, and they should move along the line of preparation that you adopted before you let it go.

At last we are ready to try a shot at the target, but all the preparation will make it easier. Stand correctly, shoulders square, but not pulled back excessively. Load the arrow onto the string, place the fingers carefully on the string, using the tab. Look up, head level. Turn the head and look calmly at the target as shown in Plate 1. Draw the bow with shoulder power in both arms and anchor under the chin as in Plate 2, making sure as you do so that the arrow is not drawn so far that it could slip inside the bow. However, this is most unlikely with the extra length of arrows you have been advised to get for that very reason. When you are satisfied on this point, come down and take the arrow off the string, re-nock it securely, stand tall, turn the head method-ically and look at the target, as in Plate 1. Draw the bow with the shoulder power and anchor under the chin as in Plate 2. Tilt the upper body so as to bring the sight pin on aim, hold it steady on aim as in Plate 3, slightly increase the string pressure on the chin by shoulder control and loose, as in Plate 4.

What happened? Maybe the arrow is in the target somewhere, or in the butt – I hope so. If it isn't, not to worry, as long as you got the arrow cleanly away. But perhaps you found some dif-ficulty. Two things in particular might have gone wrong. You may have found, as innumerable archers have before you, that the arrow fell off the ledge just as you were coming up to draw, or just before you were going to loose. If so, it was because you allowed the right hand to twist on the string and let that second finger of your right hand push the arrow off the ledge. So try again, leaving a bigger space between the arrow and the second finger. Also take care to keep the right hand flat and vertical, in line with the bow limbs. With a little perseverance you'll get the hang of it. The other thing that might have happened is that you inadvertently let the left elbow get in the way of the string as you shot it and hit your bracer or your sleeve and spoilt the shot. But if you remember the elbow position this cannot happen.

Plate 1
Preparation position, freestyle

Plate 2
Full draw, freestyle

Plate 3

Lining up the aim, freestyle

Plate 4

The loose, freestyle

If the arrows tend to miss to one side or another, try to apply equal effort in both hands, and to bring the loosing hand back off the string (as in Plate 4), instead of plucking it away from the face, which is a frequent fault in beginners. Continue to push the bow arm towards the target as the arrow is shot, and not snatch it away or downwards by clutching convulsively at the handle. Good shooting is *easy* shooting, but such easy shooting takes self-discipline and concentration.

If after repeated shooting the arrows group high, you could move the sight pin up. This will make the arrows go lower, for the sight is a front sight. If the arrows go left, you could move the pin out a bit, but not too much, because the error is much more likely to be in your release or in the lining up of the bow string, which should appear down the middle of the bow (see Plate 3). The rule on sighting is to move the sight in the direction of the error.

So far you have been shooting at one distance only, and you may well have done enough for one practice. On later occasions you will naturally want to shoot from further away, but I would recommend that you wait until you can consistently get four arrows in the 60 cm face at one time before you move 10 metres further away. Your sight will need adjusting. Mark the place where your pin has been for the first distance and then move it a finger's breadth down the bow and try that. With a little further adjustment the ideal place will be found. You should in time get sight marks for every 5 metres back to the limit you can reach shooting in this way with the bow you have.

You should vary not only the distance but also the size of the faces. Eventually the largest face should be shot at 60, 55, 50 and 45 metres, the 45 cm face shot at 45, 40, 35 and 30 metres, the 30 cm at 30, 25, 20 and 15 metres and the 15 cm face at 12, 10, 8 and 6 metres, but you will not be very likely to succeed at the longer distances with the practice bow you have. As long as you shoot the larger faces at the longer distances you can manage, and the smaller ones at closer ranges, you are observing the general intention.

A word about withdrawing the arrows. Be careful not to bend them as you withdraw them from the ground or from the target.

Press the free hand against the target so that you don't pull it over as you pull the arrow out. If you have to look behind the target for arrows, lean your bow against the front of the target. This is an accepted signal in field archery that archers are behind the target searching and it is as well if you get into the habit of it now, even if no-one is with you (see Plates 9 and 10, pp. 45 and 46).

If you do have a companion, so much the better. He can help you and you can help him to see that your positions and technique match those described or illustrated in this book. When you draw arrows from the target make sure he is not near enough to be injured if an arrow comes out of the target with a jerk, as it may do. In walking up to collect arrows take care that you do not step on his arrows or you could be called upon to pay for any you damage.

You could also score, whether on your own or with a companion, in which case it will be more competitive. Either way you will want to see how you improve from time to time – and improve you will. Write down the size of the face and the distance as well as the score. The scoring values on this type of face in FITA is 5 for spot, 4 for inner and 3 for outer.

BAREBOW

Even if you have definitely decided you want to shoot barebow, it will have done no harm, rather a great deal of good, to have worked through the method for freestyle, at any rate up to the point of shooting at one or two distances. There are so many aspects of freestyle and barebow technique which are identical or at least similar – so the inexperienced archer must refer back frequently to this section. There is another possibility, too, that later the barebow archer may decide to shoot freestyle, so some familiarity with the freestyle method is advisable. It is quite likely, on the other hand, that the reader will already be an experienced target archer, in which case he will find that his prior experience will be of great value. He can use his normal equipment as long as the bow is divested of all attachments, like sights, stabilisers, clickers or draw checks. He will handle the bow as he has been accustomed to, but he had better watch draw-length, as it is likely he may draw a longer arrow shooting barebow than he would in target archery.

The method described here is not the only one, but it is the most appropriate to teach yourself. Even if later you want to shoot 'instinctive' or semi-instinctive, that is to say, without deliberate aim, you need now to have some idea of the necessary gaps between pile and target at different distances, even if you are only aware of them without deliberate calculation. The following method will enable you to find a suitable aiming position without an instructor to tell you where to point the arrow or when you are on aim.

Before starting, set up the butt as shown before. For freestyle method it didn't matter which way up the rectangular butt was placed, but here there is a particular reason for having it set long-ways up, as will soon become clear. For the first exercise you need only one face on the target and that one only to provide an aiming mark. Fix the 15 cm Hunter face (the smallest one) at ground level, so that there is an empty expanse of target butt above it, as seen in Plate 9. If you have a sight pin on the bow, take it out and replace it in the foam or plaster strip out of sight for you are not going to use it at all. Retire about 15 metres from the target and go through the exercise to check the shoulder line, but not the head turn, for in barebow the head turn is different. Now pick up the bow and go through the elbow-locating routine.

Next, place three fingers on the string, *all three* below the nocking point, but near it. The fact that your tab has an arrow slot should be ignored. From looking down at your fingers on the string, do not raise the chin and look up as in freestyle, but turn the head angled as it is to look full face at the target. Turn the face very much more fully to the target than in freestyle. Now draw the bow by exerting the shoulders and bring the bow to the vertical position at the same time as you bend it. Let the tip of the forefinger of the string hand contact the corner of the mouth and settle firmly there, with the hand kept flat and vertical. This is the cheek anchor, the object of which is to bring the nock of the arrow, when you have one on the string, vertically below the aiming eye, but nearer to it than if you were anchoring under the chin. You should be able to observe that the string lines up with the middle of the bow limb and that the bow bisects the target vertically. If the string seems too blurred to see properly, just shut the left eye to check its position (this is an instruction for the right-handed archer). Study the position in Plates 6 and 7.

Come down and practise drawing the bow without letting go of the string, for this, you will remember, is bad for a bow, even a solid fibre-glass bow. When you can find the cheek anchor position without fumbling and can hold the bow fairly steadily at full draw, you are ready to proceed to the next exercise. Put the bow down and pick up an arrow. Hold it by the pile in the left hand and by the nock in the right hand, as if it were a rifle or shot gun, and look along the top of the shaft as if you were aiming a gun (see Plate 5). Aim it at the 15 cm face. You probably have the nock near the eye, since I mentioned a gun barrel. So now lower the nock a bit until it is at the corner of the mouth, and aim again by placing the pile of the arrow on the centre spot of the target face and observing that the shaft is pointing straight to the target. Be very sure that your eye is straight above the arrow and not canted to one side. This is how you are going to use the arrow to aim with. The head is angled to bring the aiming eye above the corner of the mouth in line with the arrow.

You will perhaps object that if the pile of the arrow is aligned with the centre of the target and you can see the shaft below eye level, the arrow will fly high at short ranges. So it will, and you are going to measure how much it rises at each distance.

First, you must practise nocking the arrow, placing three fingers below the nock and just lightly touching it with the fore-finger, and loosing into the ground as described in the freestyle method. In this way you get familiar with the action and study a good loose with a movement apart of both hands as a *result* of the release of effort, not a snatch in the *course* of loosing, which is detrimental to good shooting. Then put four arrows within easy reach, in a hip pocket for example, and take one of them, nock it and place the three fingers on the string just under the nock. Turn the head fully to look at the target. Draw smoothly and not too slowly, watching the pile of the arrow to ensure that you do not draw it past the ledge as you anchor on the

Plate 5
'Gunbarrelling' the shaft, barebow

Plate 6
Full draw, barebow

Plate 7
Full draw in profile, barebow

cheek, fore-finger at the corner of the mouth (see Plates 6 and 7). Do this a few times to satisfy yourself that the arrow is a safe length to draw and that you are in no danger of overdrawing it.

Then make sure the arrow nock is still firmly on the string (for it could have moved while you were carrying out this exercise), look calmly at the target centre spot, draw up and by adjustment from the waist if necessary, get the pile of the arrow in the middle of the spot, hold it there a moment, and loose! (See Plate 8.) If you have followed the instructions you will *not* have hit the mark aimed at, but you will see the arrow sticking in the butt some distance above it, perhaps 2 feet (60 cm) or so at this range. Shoot the other three arrows, and walk up and collect them, withdrawing the arrows as described in the freestyle method. You may have found that you flicked your nose with the string as you loosed. If so, it is a sign that you are shooting correctly but that you didn't turn your head quite fully enough to the target. If arrows have gone right or left, take care that your aiming eye is above the shaft. You can check this by seeing the string lining right along the whole length of the arrow at full draw, when the bow is upright. You may have to close, or half-close, your left eye to see this clearly, but it is only a check. Unless you have some eye problem, I want you to shoot with both eyes open, since this helps to keep the face relaxed and enables you to see better where the arrows go.

It is possible that your arrows will not be perfectly matched to the bow. It is asking a bit much with practice tackle to expect fine matching. If the arrows group a bit left or right of the vertical line above the face, you could aim off slightly, but remember that the fault could well be caused by having too stiff a bow arm, a needlessly tight grip, or most likely a loose that does not come straight back neatly off the string. Advice on loosing clean is given in the section on freestyle method, on p. 36.

Shoot again and again at this one distance until you find that the arrows are grouping reasonably well above the target face. Mark the centre of the group, as in Plate 9. Then measure the distance between the centre spot and the group and make a note of it. Now put a bigger face in the middle of the butt: it could be the biggest one, the 60 cm, or the 45 cm – you're only practising

Plate 8
The loose, barebow

Plate 9
Noting the group

Plate 10
Drawing the arrows

after all, and you deserve some encouragement. Take away the small target face. Aim the necessary distance below the centre spot of this target face and loose. You should find that you group in the target and can record a score (see Plate 10). You will notice that the 60 cm face is only a little less than 2' in diameter, that the 45 cm is only a little less than 18", that the centre spot is ⅛th of the diameter of the whole face and that the inner is half the diameter. This means you have a visual check that you can use in estimating where to place your point. When you are confident that you know what mark to use at this distance, make a note of it – you might have to amend the first note you made. Perhaps it is 2' below the spot, or 1' 8".

Whatever it is, move back 5 metres and shoot again, and so on back to 30 metres, noting the aiming marks you use. You may be surprised to find that within certain limits, say 15 – 30 metres, it doesn't matter where you stand, the aiming mark is the same. This may seem strange, but it is due to the angle of deflection being reduced by the diminishing apparent size of the face as you get further away. A look at Figure 3 will make this clear. Go further back and you will find that at longer ranges you soon have to aim closer to the target spot, exactly on it at one particular distance, and high above it at the longest distances. With your light bow you may feel disappointed that you have to aim point on or high above the target at what seems quite a short distance. Of course this is why barebow and traditional style archers like to use as powerful a bow as they can handle. But you have by no means exhausted the potential of your practice bow yet.

You will realise that you could alter your hold on the string so as to put one finger above the arrow and two below – the same hold as is used by target archers and freestylers. Incidentally, this hold is compulsory in Bowhunter and Hunting style classes. This would lower the nock of the arrow, put more elevation on the shaft and enable you to shoot at longer ranges and still have the point of your arrow conveniently near the spot on the target. Against this you would find that at short ranges you would have to aim a long way below the target. If you evolved a system of shifting the fingers up and down the string according to the

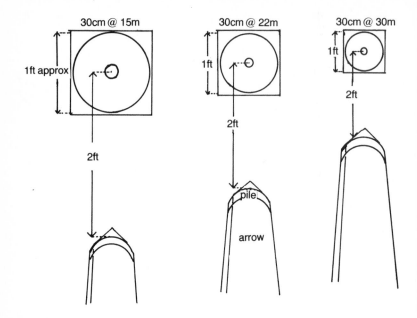

FIGURE 3   Aiming at the target

distance, you would be 'string-walking', which is allowed in the barebow class by EFAA (English Field Archery Association) but not by FITA. (See Figure 4.) Similarly, you could work out for yourself a system of different anchor-points up and down your face to match the different distances you might want to shoot. This is 'face-walking', which is allowed by EFAA in the barebow class but not by FITA (see Figure 5). Neither of these two methods is allowed by EFAA in the Bowhunter class.

For the time being it would not be wise to experiment with these systems of aiming even out of curiosity. What you could profitably do is to see which finger-hold and which anchor-point on the face gives you the best and most comfortable style. When you have decided on that, practise shooting at all the distances you can reach up to 60 metres until you have listed or memorised the marks you need to aim at, changing the faces according to the distances. Then you can try odd distances not restricted to 5

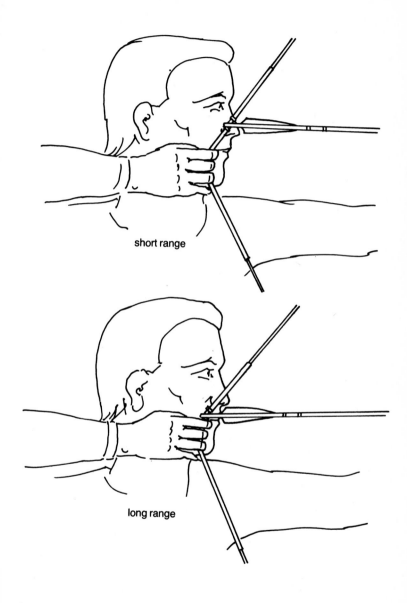

short range

long range

FIGURE 4   String walking

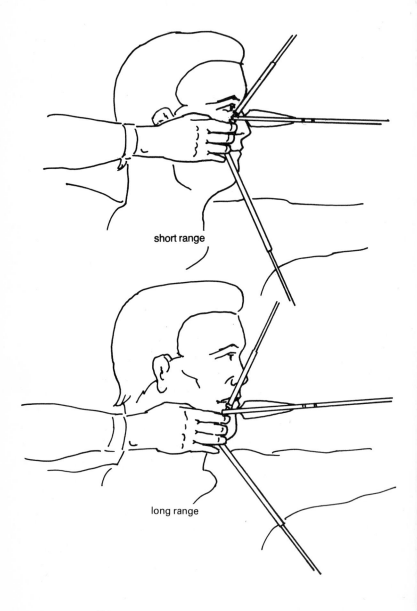

short range

long range

FIGURE 5   Face walking

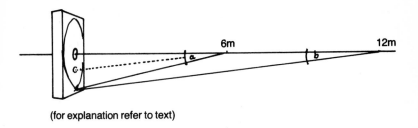

(for explanation refer to text)

FIGURE 6   Short range gapping problems

metre or 5 yard intervals. You can also try guessing or estimating the distances.

You haven't yet shot at the very short distances below 15 metres. When you do, you will find you have to aim closer to the spot than you would expect at 12, 10, 8 and 6 metres (see Figure 6). Since at such short range the arrow flight is virtually level, the same angle of aim would be required between 12 and 6 metres, yet as can be seen, the same point of aim would produce angle (a) twice as big as angle (b). If angle (b) is correct from 12 metres, then a shot from 6 metres would have to be aimed near mark (c) to be successful.

To pick up a point of aim at such close distances requires so much calculation and is so critical that most barebow archers shoot more or less instinctively at short distances even up to 30 metres. They look steadily at the spot of the target, all the time seeing the bow and the shaft in peripheral vision and when all seems to be lined up satisfactorily, they loose. It is similar to shooting a pistol from the hip – you can feel you are pointing the weapon correctly without actually aiming.

With consistent practice you would find that you could shoot this way at further and further ranges, and some barebow archers insist that they shoot instinctively at all ranges. However, you will find that at ranges where the arrow pile is necessarily pointed near the target it is very hard to ignore it and shoot by 'feel' alone, so you might as well use the point of the arrow as a reference mark at these long ranges whatever you decide to do at short ranges.

Having studied and practised either or both of these two methods, you know roughly *how* to shoot, but you are not a field archer yet, because you haven't shot over a course, nor grappled with the problems of unmarked distances. You could create a course for yourself by putting targets in various places of greater or lesser natural difficulties, but you should really try to make contact with other established field archers, or bring together like-minded enthusiasts of your own acquaintance . In the latter case you should get in touch with the governing bodies for assistance and advice.

4

EQUIPMENT

It is appropriate now to discuss the great variety of equipment that is available, not because the novice archer is recommended to dash off and buy everything in sight, but so as to inform the more experienced archer, and to prepare for the chapter on more advanced technique, which must take consideration of particular items of equipment.

All too often beginners imagine that the purchase of superior equipment will automatically bring better scores. It will if you can handle it properly, but otherwise improvement will be marginal. There is also the point that some items can be made from do-it-yourself kits or from the raw materials when you can get them. Information on this is given in Chapter 9. First, let us consider the question of whether to buy new or second-hand equipment. I have nothing against the purchase of second-hand equipment as long as the goods are sound and the price is right, bearing in mind also the loss of guarantee, and the most important proviso of all, as long as the tackle is of exactly the same specification as that which you would have bought. It often isn't.

The archer offered at a bargain price a bow 4 lbs (2 kg) heavier in draw-weight than the one he intended to get, thinks he can get used to it. Eventually he might do, especially if he makes a serious attempt at muscle-building, but in the initial period, he might easily wreck his style. I am in favour of physical improvement, but only as a prelude to using heavier tackle, or as a means of controlling existing tackle more effectively, or with the intention of promoting overall fitness. I do not recommend it as an instant cure for the over-bowed archer. You will see there are many other factors to consider in buying a tournament bow than draw-weight alone. Then again, a set of arrows in good condition may be offered, but they are 1816's whereas you really wanted 1716's. OK! They might be serviceable – you'd have to try them and see, but if the arrows won't fly properly from the bow, they are useless to you.

So we are going to consider buying new tackle unless we can find the required article second-hand, perhaps by looking in the 'Exchange and Mart' service that some go-ahead club and county organisations provide. When buying new equipment, remember that not only is a good firm unlikely to pass for sale a faulty bow, it is also jealous of its reputation and will be the more willing to rectify any fault which should occur.

BOWS

The variety is staggering. There are long-bows of the Old English type, both self-wood and laminated, solid fibre-glass, composite laminated bows, either one-piece or take-down, special hunting bows and compound bows. Cross-bows I shall not deal with, for though they have been used in field archery under the rules of some organisations, they have only recently been accepted by GNAS (Grand National Archery Society). Personally I have nothing against them, but many archers feel that the particular skill required for their use is more akin to rifle-shooting than archery in the accepted sense of the word, where the bow is held by one's own strength and released without the use of a mechanism.

THE LONG-BOW

The long-bow proper *is* long, as long as or longer than the archer using it, but it is really a name given to a typical traditional design. It will have a stirrup-shaped cross-section, be about 6 feet (1.83 m) long for a man to use, and have horn nocks. Lighter models are made for women to use, but they are of the same design, and again, each bow should be as tall as the archer using it. Whether it is made of one self-wood like yew, or with laminations of, say, hickory, greenheart and dagame, the craftsmanship will be of a high order. Some are guaranteed for a short period, such as 3 months, but as with all equipment you should examine it carefully for any flaws. A bow purchased from a manufacturer with a reputation to consider will be constructed as well as possible, and such bow-makers do not waste time and effort on poor quality materials, but there is always the possibility of accidental damage. Should you ever see a self-yew bow, you might think the humps left round small irregularities in the timber denote shoddy workmanship. Far from it; this is an essential part of creating a yew bow, the wood of which, though traditionally ideal for long-bows, often does have small blemishes that need special treatment in this way.

The bow should be evenly curved when braced and the string lined up correctly with the limbs. Regarding the draw-weight, you have to go for a fairly heavy weight in order to propel a wooden arrow a sufficient distance. The design and length of a long-bow gives a steady cast, but a much slower one than a composite bow, so you need more weight. On the other hand, the length of the long-bow does enable you to draw, hold and shoot a heavier draw-weight than you could manage in a composite. You cannot know what you can handle till you try, after having enough archery experience to 'lay the body in the bow' as medieval archers were advised, that is to say, get the shoulders doing the work rather than the arms. I will say, though, that a man using a long-bow of less than 50 lbs (23 kg) will be at a disadvantage at long ranges.

SOLID FIBRE-GLASS

As has already been explained, these are ideal for beginners' practice and club use, as you can shoot them left-handed and right-handed. They are suitable, too, for youngsters who may quickly outgrow their bows. For tournament use most people will consider their performance not quite good enough even in the heavier weights, but they are good value for money and are virtually indestructible. Some are made take-down, which means they have separate handles and limbs which can be quickly assembled and dismantled. This facility, common to all take-downs, means that a different weight of limb can be purchased without the necessity of buying an entire new bow.

COMPOSITE

The composite bow, sometimes called the 'recurve', though solid fibre-glass bows can be recurved, is used by the vast majority of archers today, target and field alike. As the name indicates, it is made of a variety of materials bonded together, usually wood and fibre-glass, or wood and carbon-fibre. Some have laminated wooden handle-sections, others aluminium or magnesium handles.

These bows get their very fine performance chiefly from the way in which light-weight wooden core materials (usually of maple-wood) are sandwiched between thin laminations of fibre-glass or carbon-fibre to oblige the latter to work efficiently. Such a bow-limb is much faster shooting than one made of solid material, whether all wood or all fibre-glass. There are many factors to consider in buying a composite. Let's deal with them one at a time.

Cost

The cost might seem to be the crucial point in selecting, but remember that there are many bows available in the same price-range, only one of which will be ideal for you. Again, you have to weigh up the respective merits of buying a cheap bow now with the intention of getting a better one later, and of buying an expensive one that is intended to last. You may change your mind later about length of limb or draw-weight. That is one reason why the take-down bow has become so popular – you *can* change the limbs.

Draw-Length

You should choose a bow made to be used at your draw-length or at a little more. A point here: to determine your true draw-length once you have learnt to shoot, you should use a measuring arrow in a bow of the same type as that which you are contemplating buying (see advice on length of arrow p. 66). If you were to use a bow even 2″ (5 cm) under-drawn you would lose the benefit not only of 1½-lb to 2 lbs (nearly 1 kg) per inch, which you can allow for, but also of the design features, which

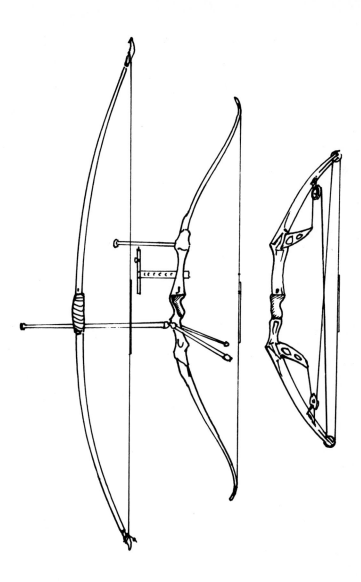

FIGURE 7   Longbow, takedown and compound bows

you can do nothing about. The loss in performance will be greater than the loss in draw-weight, for the limbs are at their most efficient when shot from a fully-flexed position. Of course, allowance must be made for growth where youngsters are concerned.

Draw-Weight

This should be a weight that you can handle efficiently, even at the end of a tiring day. You need to have learnt to shoot before you can really know what you can handle. If you are buying your first composite, take the advice of a coach or experienced archer and don't over-bow yourself. What you can hold comfortably on the fingers in the shop, you might find too much of a struggle to *shoot* properly. By all means avail yourself of any facility offered by the firm to try out bows by actually shooting them, for the bow is going to be a major item of expenditure.

If you are an experienced archer, be careful not to step up draw-weight too optimistically. You can discipline yourself to go up to 2 lbs (1 kg) all right, but 4 lbs (2 kg) would be a big jump. There is a point here whether to have limbs made of fibre-glass or carbon-fibre. The latter costs more but does produce a faster shooting bow, because of its lighter weight physically and greater tensile properties. A bow of 36 lbs (16 kg) draw-weight in carbon-fibre would probably equal the performance in feet per second of a bow of 39 lbs (18 kg) with fibre-glass limbs. Another improvement can be effected by the use of unstretchable string fibres, of which more will be discussed in Chapter 9.

TAKE-DOWN OR ONE-PIECE

The great advantage of the take-down bow is its versatility, as mentioned above, since any part, limbs or handle, can be replaced or in some cases, altered. On the other hand, some archers feel that there is an aesthetic appeal in the wooden handle riser, especially if it is laminated in exotic woods. It is possible to get take-downs with laminated wooden handle risers, but most are based on metal handles in various finishes, some, to my mind, no less attractive than wooden ones. Most wooden-handled bows are one-piece, which makes them a little more vulnerable to damage in transit than take-downs packed away in their small hold-alls. This is an important consideration when travelling by air, for one-piece bows are rarely allowed in the cabin, and therefore need to be very carefully packed to travel safely as cargo.

The laminated handle riser costs more than a self-wood handle (ie one made of one piece of wood). This is not for decoration alone; it is functional, in that the laminations give protection against any flaws, splits or warping that could occur in one piece of wood.

Weight-in-Hand

This is the physical weight of the bow. The actual effect of carrying a heavy bow round a course is not very significant, but the effect on the archer when he is using it *is* important. If a bow has a heavy handle, the mass of it will be resistant to sudden movement, so it can be held steadier. It will be less affected by outside influences, such as a somewhat 'draggy' loose, or a gust of wind. Nevertheless the weight is there, and the archer has to hold that weight, so it must not be excessive, especially if he is a freestyler and wants to add stabilisers. Magnesium risers, being lighter, are often preferred to those of aluminium alloy.

If you have never held a heavy-handled bow, you will think at first that you will not be able to hold it steady, but you will find that once drawn, the bow's physical weight seems to disappear by being distributed across the whole body, instead of hanging at the end of your out-stretched arm. Once you loose, of course, the weight is transferred to the end of the arm, but by the time this happens the arrow is away. After a few weeks you will not notice the weight-in-hand of such a bow – on the contrary, you will tend to throw a simple bow too high, having got used to the heavier one. Of course, a bow should not be so heavy in the hand that the archer starts to drop it before or at the moment of loosing, so one must keep a sense of proportion in this respect.

Length of Bow

You can say that a long composite bow will tend to be slow and

steady, and a short one will tend to be fast and more critical to
shoot, but much depends on how the bow is constructed. The
riser length is particularly significant. A bow with a long handle
riser from fade-out to fade-out, and short limbs, could be very
fast if drawn fully. A bow with a very short handle section and
average limbs could be quite steady.

Freestylers mostly go for the kind of bow dimensions used by
target archers. Barebow archers favour bows that are shorter and
faster. With their style of shooting the bow can be shorter in the
handle riser and have a shorter sight-window. Archers using
wooden arrows may desire even greater power, for wooden
arrows are heavier than alloy, and accordingly choose a bow
designated as a hunting bow, even if it is not used for that
purpose. It is very short, perhaps as short as 58″ (1.47 m), and
probably has a draw-weight of more than 46 lbs (21 kg) for a
man. There are often very pronounced recurves at the tips of the
limbs to give extra speed. Some archers choose the hunting bow
just because they like to associate field archery with hunting.

Handle Shape

By this I mean the actual 'grip', though I would rather not use
that word, since the bow should be held lightly. This should not
only feel a convenient size for your hand, but also set your wrist
in the way you like to hold it when shooting. Some archers like a
high wrist, others a low wrist. A semi-pistol 'grip' is likely to suit
most people. Preferably the handle wants to be fairly slender in
the 'throat' as you are then less likely to apply pressure in the
wrong place than with a chunky thick handle. For obvious
reasons a handle of metal may be made more slender than of
wood. Some manufacturers supply a variety of clip-on 'grips' to
suit the standard take-down model.

Length and Depth of Cut-out or Sight Window

The side of the bow limb against which the arrow rests before it
is shot is cut away so as to allow the arrow to lie along the
centre-line of the bow, and this cut-out extends up the bow to
afford a clear view of the target. It is important for the freestyler
that this cut-out allows him to put his sight up far enough to sight

at 5 metres. The barebow archer has no such problems.

Many bows are now made so that the cut-out is past the centre line. This allows a clear view of the target and more latitude on sight movement, and also allows for the fitting of an adjustable arrow-rest, one that can be wound in or out to suit the behaviour of the arrow shafts currently in use. Where barebow archers are allowed to use them, they may at least have to immobilise them for the duration of a tournament, but they are very handy to set up the bow for ideal arrow flight.

Stabiliser Bushes

With a wooden handle riser, quite often bushes can be put in later if required. On a metal handle riser it is as well to see that such bushes are provided wherever you may later require them, eg top and bottom for 'twins', centre for poker, long-rod or V-bar system, inside of the top of the riser for compensating weight. You might at first decide you don't want stabilisers and then change your mind later, or choose one system and then want to change to another, you see. If you wish to use TFC's (torque flight compensators, or dampers), which minimise the shock effect of the stabilisers, keep in mind that you might not always wish to fit a stabiliser at those particular points. Should you have an excess number of such attachments you might be obliged to remove one or two of them, which could be difficult. With the barebow archer I cannot be so specific. Some organisations like EFAA allow stabilisers in Barebow Class (as long as they are not usable as sighting aids), but not in Bowhunter and Hunting Style. FITA and GNAS don't allow them at all in the Barebow or Traditional Classes. So you will be pleased to find stabiliser bushes in a bow or be indifferent about it, according to your organisation or class.

Built-in TFC's could cause problems to the barebow archer in FITA or GNAS, as exception could be taken not only to the flexible core (or damper proper) even though it does not accommodate a stabiliser rod, but also to the mounting surrounding it. The core can easily be removed; the mounting perhaps not so easily.

Finish

A good finish adds to the appearance and protects the bow.

Tiller and Alignment

Look at the bow when braced. It should look symmetrical with just a suggestion of a little more stiffness in the lower limb, barely noticeable to anyone but an expert. This tiller is intended to allow for the points of pressure on the bow handle and on the string being below centre, (below the arrow at any rate). Then look along the string from both ends while the bow is braced to see if the limbs are straight. Occasionally a bow may show a lean to one side or the other at the tips. If so, don't accept it, for it may get worse with use, until finally the string won't stay on it.

Freedom from Stack

Try drawing the bow. A good bow should feel easy on the last few inches of draw. If you notice a fierce build-up of resistance as you come to full draw, you have a bow which 'stacks'. Choose one that feels fairly smooth. If you can try the bow before committing yourself to purchase, do so.

COMPOUND BOWS

After some resistance by users of 'conventional' bows, the compound bow is now firmly established. It makes brilliant use of two new concepts in bow-making, a block and tackle pulley system, and eccentric wheels at the limb tips. The former provides an easier draw since the very powerful limb tips have to move less per length of string travel, the tips moving only about 3″ (8 cm) against the 8″ (20 cm) or so, of a composite. This means, too, that there is less inertia to overcome on release as the limbs move less, producing a faster cast.

The eccentric wheels provide more leverage at the limb tips as the bow approaches full draw, so that the bow requires the major effort in drawing part-way through its string movement and eases off before reaching full draw. Once over the 'hump' of peak poundage the bow is easy to be drawn full and held. This has two valuable effects:

1   It enables the archer to hold on aim extremely steadily.

Incidentally, exact draw-length is not so critical because less power per inch is exerted at this point.

2 Since the arrow accelerates as it approaches the bow from a relatively slow and low-powered start, a lighter shaft can be used. This travels faster than a heavy one. It need not be so stiff either. If the bow is loosed with the fingers, the spine of the arrow can be that which would suit a composite bow of poundage half-way between the peak weight of the compound and its holding weight. To give a clearer illustration, a shaft suiting a 42 lbs (19 kg) composite would suit a compound tuned to a peak weight of 50 lbs (23 kg) and a holding weight of 34 lbs (15 kg). If a release device is used then the arrow suitable for a composite bow of 34 lbs could be used for the compound peaking at 50 lbs. Its performance would be of a bow of considerably greater poundage than a composite of 50 lbs, for it makes better use of stored energy.

Care should be taken in selecting the compound to suit you personally, and getting it set up for your draw-length, draw-weight and shooting characteristics, but for that, you should read the specialist literature on the subject and the makers' brochures and handbooks. Compounds aren't cheap: they cannot be with so much expertise and many specially-engineered parts, but then a good composite is not cheap either. A lower-priced compound with fewer moving parts is based on a simplified design and is appropriately called a 'two-wheeler'. This is said to be permanently in tune. Actually it cannot be adjusted much for draw-length or draw-weight, but most archers do not vary much in their requirements in these respects. The more elaborate models, however, can be adjusted within fine limits to give ideal performances. Perfect scores have been shot with these bows. After all this, it may come as a blow to learn that not all organisations accept them. At the time of writing, FITA does not, and GNAS does (but not in direct competition with 'conventional' bows), NFAS (National Field Archery Society) accepts them in the Unlimited class, and EFAA in all classes except Barebow proper, but with certain conditions for each.

The compound bow is still a controversial item, both its supporters and its denigrators holding and expressing extreme, and no doubt sincere, views. The fact is, man has been trying for thousands of years to improve on the simple instrument – and has succeeded in all sorts of ways, especially in the last half-century. The compound is the first bow to make use so dramatically of an improvement upon basic principles. But many archers will still wish to 'do it the hard way'. At one extreme this means using a long-bow and wooden arrows. In between are the vast numbers of ordinary archers interested in all types of barebow and freestyle who accept, according to their individual choice, some of the benefits of modern technology (like fibre-glass and carbon-fibre laminations) while denying themselves others (such as the spirit-level) as being either within or outside their personal concept of what constitutes 'real' archery.

ARROWS

To put it briefly, arrows may be made of wood, natural or compressed, or of aluminium alloy or fibre-glass tubing. Research is constantly being made into new materials.

With wooden arrows, as with any other articles made of natural material, close matching is difficult to achieve. Wooden shafts of the same length and cross-section may vary widely in weight, spine (stiffness), springiness (not necessarily the same thing as stiffness) and balance – not to say, straightness! Since they must also be fletched with feathers, yet another variable due to use of natural materials is introduced. Nevertheless, with great care a very good set of matched wooden arrows can be made, but nowhere near as uniform as can be produced with alloy shafts and plastic vanes. True, an archer can allow for individual peculiarities in particular arrows, but this creates extra problems – there is enough to think about without that. Since wooden arrows are obligatory in some sections (eg GNAS Traditional, NFAS and EFAA Hunting Style) you may need to buy or make some.

Fibre-glass arrows always stay straight and are very strong, but they can shatter under extreme stress. They tend to be heavier than alloy shafts. There is less variety of specification available than there is in alloy. For these and other reasons, almost all archers using shafts other than wooden ones choose aluminium alloy shafts and these very largely from tubing made by one shaft manufacturer, though the completion of the fletching is often done by other suppliers.

Factors to consider are quality of shaft, length, spine, weight, type of pile, type of nock, type and size of fletching, and finish. It will be most convenient to deal with both wooden and alloy arrows under these headings. Information on the assembling of alloy arrows from the parts that can be bought is also given later, but here we are concerned chiefly with purchase.

This chapter deals only with bought goods, but you will find that the majority of archers using woods make up their own arrows from the basic materials (see Chapter 9).

Quality of Shaft

Only one timber is really acceptable for wooden field arrows, and that is Port Orford cedar, for it is reasonably straight-grained, fairly light yet quite strong and can be worked easily. It is sometimes possible to get shafts made of compressed cedar, with greater density towards the pile end, which gives extra strength and a more forward point of balance, but most archers use selected natural cedar shafts.

With alloy, too, you have to pay for excellence, the more expensive shafts being harder, tougher and more finely matched. You will find that different grades of the same dimensions will have slightly different spine characteristics, due to different alloys and processing alterations, but the suppliers' charts make all this clear. If you are still liable to miss the butt often, you had better go for relatively inexpensive arrows, for an expensive arrow is just as easily lost as a cheap one. Of course, with a good firm's products you can get other shafts identical with any you lose, which cannot be done to the same degree of accuracy with some of the very cheap alloys obtainable, even when replacements are advertised. The better quality shafts are all resistant to permanent bends – and any bends that do occur can usually be straightened out with the aid of a straightening tool and gauge, unless they have a dent or kink in them.

Length

As wooden field arrows are usually fitted with a field pile which is over-sized (ie it fits over the shaft and not flush with it) it is usual to draw the arrow up to the pile and leave the pile projecting beyond the rest (or hand, with a long-bow). So the measurement of length is from the slot of the nock to the place where the wooden shaft meets the metal sleeve of the pile.

An alloy arrow, unless it has a field pile, which is unlikely, is measured from the slot of the nock to the shoulder of the pile (ie the junction of the taper and the parallel part of the pile itself). The arrow should be of a length that you can just draw through a clicker, if you use one. If you don't, you still don't want any excess length, for it adds extra weight. If you shoot barebow, then you could use the same length as above in order to be able to observe when it is full drawn. You can have it a little longer if you prefer, so as to see the pile a little more easily as your aiming aid, or to be confident of not drawing the arrow off the rest or ledge if you use a fast action and ignore the view of the arrow, as some instinctive archers do.

Remember that the length and stiffness interact. An arrow 1″ longer than another of the same specification will be more 'whippy' and have less spine (that is, it'll bend more).

Spine

Before discussing spine, one must explain what happens when an arrow is loosed from the fingers. When the force required to hold the bow at full draw is released, it moves the nock end of the arrow before it affects the pile end. You might think the arrow would minutely shorten along its length and remain straight. Not so. Since the string always slides round the finger ends as the loose is achieved, the direction of thrust is such that the arrow first bends inwards into the bow, then the natural resilience of the shaft coupled with the wave-like motion of the string causes it to bend outwards. By this time it should be mid-way past the arrow-pass (where the arrow-rest is) and *not* touching bow or rest. Next it bends back again in front of the bow, the nock just clearing the bow as the arrow, still oscillating, speeds on its way to the target. The fletching rapidly damps down the oscillations to produce steady flight. This behaviour of the arrow is called the 'archer's paradox' since it once seemed illogical that an arrow could go straight to the target while apparently being shot off the side of the bow. Now, if the bending qualities of the arrow do not match the speed at which it passes the bow, if any of its movements are out of phase, then poor arrow flight will ensue. One way of roughly expressing these bending qualities is in terms of spine.

In about 1950 GNAS decided to standardise the measurement of arrow stiffness by measuring the deflections (in what were called GNAS spine units) of one-hundredths of an inch when a 1½-lb weight was hung on the mid-point of an arrow while it was supported at the extremities. So an arrow deflecting, say 52 one-hundredths of an inch is stiff; while one deflecting, say 67 one-hundredths, is whippy.

Just to complicate matters, the American AMO measurement of spine is determined by measuring the deflection in decimal points of an inch when a 2 lbs weight is suspended on an arrow supported 1″ short of the extremities. So the readings are different. Thus 0.700″ AMO= 59 GNAS, and 0.775″ AMO = 65 GNAS. However, conversion tables are provided by the bigger manufacturers, so there is no real problem here. But remember the reading is dependent on the length of the arrow.

Sometimes the spine value of wooden field arrows is not stated, but instead they are guaranteed to be suitable for certain weights of bow, which means that they have been spined. Fine spine-matching of wooden arrows is not really feasible, for they are more liable to be affected by atmospheric conditions than alloy shafts. Another point is that the wooden shaft will bend more across the grain than on the edge of it. True, the cock feather is set on the edge of the grain, or should be, but there is still a variable. Light bows will need a $5/16$″ shaft, while heavier ones will need $11/32$″.

With alloy arrows another standardisation is universally recognised in terms of outside diameter of shaft measured in sixty-fourths of an inch, and wall-thickness of tube measured in one-thousandths of an inch. So you might have a 'barge-pole' of a shaft identified as a 2016, meaning it measures $20/64$″ outside diameter and $^{16}/_{1000}''$ wall-thickness, or a 'knitting-needle' type of arrow shaft of 1416 specification $^{14}/_{64}''$ outside diameter and $^{16}/_{1000}''$ wall-thickness. Since there is a range of both diameters and wall-thicknesses, you can see that there are a great many combinations possible, and even that similar-spined arrows can be available in more than one shaft size. A number of different shafts could suit the same bow. What you use depends on what you want.

Take some standard wall-thicknesses: $^{13}/_{1000}''$ is thin and produces a light shaft that will give you greater cast and distance of value to you if you use a light bow. On the other hand the light shaft is liable to be more affected by the wind. A $^{16}/_{1000}''$ shaft is going to be heavier in the same diameter, but it will be less liable to accidental damage. $^{18}/_{1000}''$ shafts will be even more durable though heavier still. They will be less affected by the wind and can be shot with advantage by a heavy bow. The above summary is a simplification. Since the light shafts travel faster, this to some extent reduces possible effect of cross-winds.

So quality of material, length of shaft, wall-thickness and overall diameter all affect spine. The performance of an arrow when shot is also affected by the weight of the pile, the type and size of the fletching, and your style of shooting. I have already explained how the method of shooting the compound bow off the fingers or with a release affects the spine of arrow required. The amount by which a bow is made centre-shot affects the spine, too. Clearly, then, there are many things to consider in selecting a set of arrows to suit you and your bow. There are, admittedly, some adjustments to plunger buttons that can make various spined arrows shoot efficiently from the bow, but you do want to get the best match available. So study the charts provided by the makers whose advice is very sound, and then, if you can, try out in actual practice the test sets that top-class suppliers provide for trial on their testing ranges by prospective purchasers.

Weight

Wooden arrows are heavier than alloys. This is one of the reasons why archers using them often use heavier poundage bows. One is governed by the spine and thickness of shaft that will suit the bow being used. With alloys there is a little more choice in that by selecting a certain tube size you could, if you wanted, have the same spine in a heavier arrow. Certainly much closer matching for weight can be guaranteed.

The weight of an arrow is expressed in grains; thus a 28″ alloy arrow of 354 grains is heavy while a 28″ alloy arrow of 280 grains is light. To decide whether to use a heavy or light arrow, when either will otherwise suit the bow, there are a few points to consider. The heavy arrow will have a lower initial velocity than the lighter one, but it will maintain its speed better. The speed of the lighter arrow will 'fade' more quickly. Travelling at the same velocity the heavier arrow will stick in harder, but then the lighter arrow would be travelling faster – it depends how far away the target is. Seeing that field targets are set at relatively short ranges, it probably makes little difference with alloys. Wooden arrows certainly do lose range rapidly at the longer distances, though this is partly due also to the size of the feather fletching. Stability in strong winds is a more valid reason for preferring heavy arrows. You could add that they are less likely to be deflected by hitting a leaf or twig where the target offers a not quite clear shot.

Type of Pile

On wooden field arrows the piles are usually field piles, which have a kind of double taper at the point, enabling good penetration into the target without allowing the arrows to drive too deeply into the soil or undergrowth if they should miss the target. It is best if they are over-size (that is to say, if they are a little bigger than the shaft over which they fit without necessitating reduction of the shaft, which would weaken it.)

Piles are available in more than one weight, for in some bowhunter classes a pile of a certain minimum weight must be used, say, 125 grains for men or 100 for ladies, to equate with the assumed weight of a broadhead that would be used when actually hunting with the bow. A similar weighted type of pile is designed for alloy shafts, too. Most alloy arrows for field shooting, though, are fitted with piles of exactly the same shape and weight as those used by target archers. Some advanced field and target archers go a step further to improve on the standard piles and use heavier weight piles, 20 grains heavier than standard, because they feel they will give finer bow-tuning and a more forward point of balance. Some heavy-weight piles are available as bullet-piles, which give better penetration than the more common conical pile. For economical production reasons heavy-weight piles for alloy arrows are not available in every listed shaft size, but only in the more popular ones.

Type of Nock

Here again there is no little variety. Wooden arrows are frequently nocked with plastic index nocks, the index guide being a rib that can be felt with the thumb while taking an arrow from a shoulder quiver. The rib is in line with the cock-feather, so the arrow can be nocked on the string without the necessity of looking at it. Alloy arrows have the same nocks available as for target arrows. Currently, the snap-on type are popular as they can be securely put on the string and yet be released with freedom on loose. The string can rotate within the 'eye' of the nock without coming free by accident. Such nocks are a boon to those archers who shoot with three fingers under the arrow, as nocks with straight-sided slots can come adrift using this method. Some of these designs also have an index guide that can be felt while preparing to nock the arrow on the string.

Do be at some pains to see that the nocks are all identical in size of slot. If a set of arrows have unevenly-sized nock slots, some are going to travel more slowly than others on loose, because of the 'pluck-back' of the string before the arrow gets free. But in using a good make there is no fear of this.

Type and Size of Fletching

Feather-fletching is customary on wooden arrows and is obligatory in some classes. It is usually two-coloured to provide a quick identification of cock-feather. For wooden arrows the fletchings will usually be 4″ or bigger, and may be off-set or spiralled round the shaft to give better direction by spinning the arrow more than it would do so otherwise, for owing to the nature of natural feather even straight-fletched arrows with feather-fletching will spin. If excessive, though, off-set fletching or spiral fletching will cause too much drag and the arrows will drop short, especially at long ranges. Alloy and fibre-glass arrows may be fletched with feathers, but generally plastics are used. They are smaller than those used on wooden arrows and of a size appropriate to the size and length of the shaft, varying from, say, 1¾" (45 mm) in length to 3½" (90 mm). They are more uniform than feathers and are not affected by rain, these being two main reasons for their use.

Personal taste is largely the reason why some archers choose rigid vanes, others flexible ones, and others again the slotted type which mimic in some degree the behaviour of feathers. Rigid vanes probably give the most undeviating arrow flight, but are more liable to suffer damage in the target and again the archer must ensure that they do not touch the bow when the arrow is loosed. The flexible ones are less easily dislodged or broken, but can become bent or twisted. The slotted ones can also become twisted in use, especially if they are put on with an off-set. They travel a little slower than solid plastics, but faster than feathers. Generally the advantages and disadvantages compensate each other with all of these.

Shapes vary, too, it is the total area that matters, rather than length or height in themselves. Shield and parabolic shapes are most common. The long low-profile shapes are also used, since the arrow is then less likely to be diverted by their touching leaves or twigs. Colour of fletching is a factor of some importance, for the field archer needs to be able to see where his arrows go. In FITA on marked distance rounds he may use binoculars, but on unmarked distances he may not do so – yet he does need to *see* the arrows to make any necessary adjustments to sight, point of aim, or gap. Unfortunately, there is only a small range of fluorescent colours. Some archers use a strip of rabbit-fur glued just behind the fletching to produce a star-burst effect as the arrow hits the target and the tiny hairs fan out with the impact. But they could be obliged to use fur-fletched arrows for all shots at that target, and fur does cause extra drag on the arrows, more at the long distances than at the short, so its use is not very common.

One thing you can consider is the colour of the target. Fletchings coloured so that they stand out on a nearly all-black Hunter face would not be so distinguishable on a coloured Forester face, and so on. Depending on what rounds you most often shoot, you will choose your most distinguishable colour.

With target archers, variations on fletching angles and numbers of fletching are not infrequently seen, but in field archery the standard three fletchings set at 120 degrees to each other are used by nearly all archers. Such two-fletched designs as I have seen would appear to be far too vulnerable to damage in the target for field use.

Finish

Lastly we come to the question of finish. Wooden arrows need to be protected against the weather by varnish or some other sealer. Dampness in the atmosphere alone can cause wooden arrows to warp. A constant humidity should be retained in the timber, to prevent it getting sluggish when wet, or brittle when over-dry. So apart from protection against rain, a good sealer is necessary. Alloy shafts will deteriorate if neglected, but if wiped after use and kept polished should not give any trouble. However, the anodised finishes now provided on the better alloy arrows give excellent protection as well as enhancing the appearance. A minor point is that the non-glare effect prevents one being dazzled to quite the same extent when aiming at a target at high elevation with the sun behind it, should you reach that part of the course at such an unlucky time.

BOW-CASE

In order to protect the bow when not in use, it should be kept in a bow-case, preferably padded. An unlined bow-bag is useful but does not afford the same protection. Take-downs usually have their own hold-all provided as part of the equipment.

TACKLE BOX

Certainly a container to hold the arrows and a great deal of other equipment securely is needed. Some of the most convenient arrow-racks are those simply made of foam rubber with slots cut in them. Into these, arrows may be pressed so as to travel safely separated from each other, whereas in the more usual wooden arrow racks the arrows tend to rattle. In getting a box, consider having it roomy enough for all the other gear you may accumulate.

BRACER

Some archers don't use bracers, arguing that only a bad archer hits his bow-arm with the string. But this is not necessarily true. If someone has a very loose hold on the bow – no bad thing at all – the string can sting the arm after loose. Again, the bracer is useful to keep any loose clothing on the arm out of the way of the string. Whether made of leather or plastic, the bracer should be comfortable to wear, perhaps a skeleton or perforated design for hot weather, and stiff enough not to become misshapen after some months of use. Most archers will find one which covers the fore-arm sufficient. See that it is not so long that it chafes the wrist when the hand is bent inwards. You may prefer a bracer which covers both the lower and upper arm, but it must not restrict the bending movement of the elbow, nor should it be bought merely because you haven't bothered to locate the elbow properly in the sideways position and want to guard against flogging the elbow-joint with the string. If you are left-handed see that the buckles or other fittings are conveniently placed for you to do them up with the left hand, because some, being made for right-handers, are awkward to handle.

TAB OR SHOOTING-GLOVE

Tabs are made of leather or man-made alternatives. The latter are not necessarily inferior – for one thing they are waterproof. If you suffer from soreness and callouses on the pads of one or more fingers you may think a double-thickness tab will help. So it will, but you'll lose some sensitivity. Your trouble could be due to faulty technique. Much the same applies to soreness on the inside of the fore-finger caused by pinching the arrow at full draw, especially with a short bow. Well, there are tabs with finger-spacers, but again, it's worth checking over your technique first. There are some tabs made of leather or seal-skin with the hair left on. This gives a fast clean loose, even in wet weather, but eventually the hair wears off.

Archers who habitually shoot with three fingers under the arrow do not need a nock slot in the tab, and often make a simplified design to suit themselves. Some use shooting gloves, in which the finger ends at least are protected with leather finger stalls. As long as the glove is close-fitting and cannot slip, these can be serviceable, but you cannot get as sharp a loose with a glove as you can with a tab.

QUIVER

Archers using wooden arrows often go in for the back-quiver, tooled in leather with hunting knife and pocket for spares. These are certainly suitable, for they hold a lot of arrows, which the traditionalist needs to have. On the other hand it is not too easy to see which arrow you are withdrawing, if you should want to select a particular one; the rain can run down and saturate the inside of the quiver, and you can spill some of the arrows or catch the nocks in overhanging branches, by bending down carelessly.

The simple belt quiver, whether flat or tubular, as used by some target archers, is not very convenient, for it is usually designed to hold only about six arrows. The most convenient, certainly for those using alloy arrows, is the holster quiver which is big enough to hold some spare arrows, as well as those currently in use. A keeper strap retains those that are spare or discarded temporarily for repairs. The angle at which they are held enables one to pass through bracken or close woodland with ease.

BOW-SLING

Since the bow performs best when it is held loosely, very many archers, freestyle and barebow alike, use a bow-sling. The design is immaterial, as long as it holds the bow securely after loose, and is adjustable so that the archer's hand and wrist are not constricted at full draw. With a sling, the bow need not be grasped at all, as it can find its own best position in the hand, and is free to function properly. A finger-sling joining thumb and forefinger may be sufficient for some bows that are light in the hand.

You can pay a lot of money for a sight; for field archery it is important to have one that can be easily adjusted within fine limits. In general, the target archer sets his sight for a given distance, and, having adjusted it to his satisfaction, tends to leave it alone for quite a long time while he shoots several dozen arrows. The distances are usually in tens of yards or metres. But the freestyle field archer may need to reset his sight before shooting every arrow on a Hunter Round, and certainly at least once on every target in the Field Round. Furthermore, the distances required can vary between 5 yards or 5 metres and 70 yards or 60 metres. He may need to have marks set for both yards and metres.

For these reasons it seems best to me to have a sight which allows for direct distances marking on to the scale, rather than one which is calibrated in inches or centimetres. It takes longer and can cause error to find a sight-marking by reference to a card showing distances related to a scale on the bow. Micrometer-type fittings for vertical and lateral adjustment are very convenient, because a very small shift of the sight, which is relatively near to the eye, makes a big difference on the target. The shape and design of the aperture should suit the eyesight of the archer using it, and be in accordance with the rules applicable to the round being shot. If allowed, a spirit-level near the sight is of great help on slopes (or even on level ground), but FITA and GNAS do not allow a levelling device of any kind.

Where you position your sight depends in part on where you can focus conveniently. A sight on the face side of the bow (the side facing you) is not recommended because it could be claimed that you could use the sight-markings as well as the sight itself to gauge distance. It is better to fix the sight track on the far side of the bow, where it is then still easy to read and adjust without letting go of the handle. Very much in the fore just now are side-mounted sights on a bracket which permits the sight to project from 6″ (15 cm) to 20″ (50 cm) towards the target. One could argue that such an apparatus functions as a stabiliser, and so it does, but its real purpose is to extend the distance between eye and sight to get greater accuracy of aim. This it will do, but only if you can hold it steady.

You must take care that the sight-pin or aperture is not put in such a position that the arrow hits it when it is shot. It is feasible to shoot the arrow over instead of under the sight, but one is not so likely to want to do this on field courses as one might do at long range in a target shoot. In any case, the length of the projection is adjustable, so that an ideal position may be found where it can stay for all ranges. Some forward sight tracks are set at an angle, so that for close ranges the sight is further away from the eye than it is at longer ranges. This is quite a good idea, as the track can be calibrated quite as easily as a vertical one, yet give a sighting advantage where it can be used most effectively.

THE STRING PEEP

Though not allowed in FITA, the peep sight is allowed by other organisations in some freestyle classes. It is often used with compounds where it complements the use of a release. In effect, it is a back sight located on the string, giving a small aperture through which the front sight on the bow is aligned with the target, giving extra accuracy of aim.

CLICKER OR DRAW-CHECK

A draw-check can be any device used to verify when the arrow is full drawn, whether visual or aural. In some classes, of course, they will be banned, but where they are allowed they can be very useful, for an arrow half an inch underdrawn may lose velocity of 7 feet (2.13 m) per second, which could be significant in itself, quite apart from the loss of form which the underdraw exposes.

Those who use clickers sometimes use them as draw-checks, pure and simple; the majority use them as an audible signal of when to loose. Various designs are available. It is advantageous to use one which can be adjusted easily for length of draw and for strength of spring (a stronger spring producing a more audible signal).

In some classes (like EFAA Barebow) an under-arrow clicker

is permitted so there can be no question of its being used as an aiming aid. Even those using sights might find an under-arrow clicker convenient, so as to avoid having anything in the bow window but the sight.

KISSER

The dimensions of an attachment to the string for the freestyler are regulated by the rules of the various organisations; in some cases this may be 1 cm, in others ⅜". Such an attachment can serve as a lip or nose mark, but not as an eye mark. It is usually drawn to a point between the lips (hence its popular name), but it could equally well be drawn to some other sensitive location, eg the nose or corner of the mouth in a cheek anchor for freestyle.

Since most freestylers draw three fingers under the chin, one finger being over the arrow, you might think a kisser hardly necessary, but it does in fact serve in lieu of a back sight to ensure that the nock of the arrow is the same distance below the aiming eye on every shot, uniformity in this respect being vital in aiming. If the side anchor is used, the kisser may be located at the corner of the mouth. In this way a longer arrow may be drawn, and some archers, target as well as field, find it helps to get the shoulders into the bow.

ARROW-REST

Unless the arrow is shot off the hand as with the long-bow, or off a ledge that forms part of the bow, a rest is needed. If plastic fletching is used a rest is essential. There are many designs, but the important feature is to support the arrow safely while it is being shot, and not to get in the way of the arrow or fletchings as it passes.

ADJUSTABLE ARROW-REST

To get the very best results in arrow performance it is frequently necessary to be able to align the shaft straight down the centre of the bow, or a little to left or right of it, depending on arrow spine and the archer's technique, and left or right-handedness. This can be done if a moveable arrow-plate is fitted on the riser, and adjusted by a milled nut or other fitting on the side away from the arrow. The arrow-rest proper is stuck on this plate. Another way of moving the arrow slightly left or right of the centre line is by using a plunger-button. This often has two adjustments: one to move the button in or out, and the other to regulate the tension in the spring-loading of the button to harden or soften its action. The arrow bears against this button while it is being shot. Either adjustment will assist in fine tuning of the bow and arrow. Occasionally both will need to be attended to in setting up a bow for a particular set of arrows, or archer.

STABILISERS

Where these are allowed, as in FITA Freestyle, and EFAA Free-style and Barebow, the behaviour of the bow on loose can be controlled. If an unstabilised bow is shot by a finger-loose it will tend to torque or rotate in the hand. The addition of rods or small weights extended from the riser will obviously reduce this effect. The object is to make the bow retain after loose the attitude it had before loose.

You have the choice of various systems. One is to have a long-rod projecting, say, 14" (35 cm) to 30" (76 cm) in front of the bow. This will reduce torque but tend to make the bow dip forward on loose. Alternatively you could use 'twins', one at the top, and one at the bottom of the riser. These could be shorter and have the same anti-torque effect without so much forward tip on loose. A small counter-weight could be fitted inside top or bottom limb to counteract the forward weight of the long-rod or twins. Lastly, you could have a V-bar system located just below the hand-hold. This would provide a forward-pointing long-rod with two smaller rods projecting backwards, but angled away from the string. The latter counter-balances the weight of the long-rod. By this means the bow is rendered very stable indeed, and retains exactly the same attitude as it had before loose. Target archers sometimes adjust the angle of the twin-rods to settle the sight on the target at the particular distance about to be shot, and change it for each distance – but field archers cannot do this, as it would be impractical when distances of targets are perpetually changing. So they find the best compromise suitable for all distances.

TORQUE FLIGHT COMPENSATORS

Torque flight compensators or dampers are attachments fitted between stabilisers and bows. Since they are slightly flexible, they allow the bow to move slightly so as to allow the arrow to pass naturally without counteracting the anti-torque action of the stabilisers. If no TFC's are used, the extra mass of the stabilisers added to the bow will tend to affect arrow-flight, though not necessarily to any critical extent.

RELEASE

Releases are of various kinds. They are not allowed by FITA, neither by GNAS except conceivably where a physically disabled archer could not shoot without one. But they have their place, especially for users of compound bows, some of which perform much better when loosed with a release, since there is less 'wander' of the string after loose. The whole idea of the release is to enable the string to travel as directly as possible straight to the point where the arrow leaves the string without the wave-like motion that is unavoidable with a finger-loose. Assuming you wish to control the loose, you will ignore those that release 'on surprise', but there is still a variety operating by different systems, such as trigger or rotation methods. It would be well to try out which suit you best before purchase, as some can be expensive.

BINOCULARS

Where binoculars are permitted as in FITA on marked distances, you need to consider magnification, field of vision, lightness in weight, and, of course, price. It is no use having a pair of binoculars with 20x magnification, for you could not hold them steady. Even 10x or 12x are hard to hold steady with two hands, and if you wanted to view the target with one hand in the bow sling and the other holding the binoculars, you might find that 7x or 8x are as powerful as you can hold steady.

With binocular specifications the first figure is magnification, the second the diameter of the object glass, in millimetres. If you have a high magnification and a relatively small object glass, say

16x40 you will have poor luminosity, a narrow field of vision, and have trouble in holding it steady. If you have a modest magnification and a relatively large object glass, say 7x50, you will have good luminosity, a wide field of vision, and be able to hold very steady. The body of the binoculars might be a little heavy, though. All things considered, for most people 8x40 will do very well for field archery where distances are not so great as in target archery. 10x50 could be even better if you have a steady hand. Light-weight models are to be preferred to heavy ones, as the lightness helps one to hold steady.

Binoculars are really useful in field archery, for it is an advantage to know where the first arrow has gone in case it may be necessary to adjust sights (especially on severe slopes where normal sight marks might not be quite right). On the other hand, a good many field archers will consider them anathema, arguing that a hunter would use them to spot game, but not to verify whether he'd hit the quarry or not.

CLOTHING

Obviously this depends on weather conditions generally. But a close-fitting upper garment, trousers and stout shoes or boots are advisable. To stand without slipping on steep slopes, or to climb slopes, golf shoes are useful, so too are light rubber boots with rubber-studded soles. Gum-boots are rather tiring to wear and let twigs enter, much to the archer's irritation. Certainly one must consider wet weather and have light-weight waterproofs that can be carried round the course, if it seems necessary. They should be so designed as to allow access to pockets underneath, and to allow reasonable freedom of action when shooting.

The sleeveless tunic or jerkin is particularly useful in cold weather, since it does not impede the arms. A shirt-guard might seem an ultra-refinement, but if either men or women find that the string is liable to catch on clothing near the chest or shoulder, they can wear a shirt-guard to prevent that happening. Some nylon waterproofs are necessarily roomy in the chest, and need keeping back out of the way of the string. For use in wet weather I would recommend vinyl or nylon mesh shirt-guards rather than leather ones, since they won't absorb water. They are cool in hot weather, too.

OTHER ACCESSORIES

You might well include a sheath-knife for prising reluctant piles out of tree-trunks or wooden target supports. Another essential tool is the rake, a single-pronged hook to draw through the soil or undergrowth in the hope of locating buried arrows. Some means of carrying small items of equipment, such as a spare arrow-rest, spare string, nocks, glue, and so on, needs to be provided, for once out on the course the field archer cannot conveniently return to his tackle box for repairs. Some quivers have pockets for such small items, or a small purse-like case can be attached to the belt.

5
CLASSES OR STYLES

This chapter will briefly outline the different classes or styles of shooting. To go into too much detail would be tedious, and as there is always the possibility of rule changes the archer is advised to refer to the current rule book of his association for fuller and more up-to-date information. It will be convenient to deal with the classes under the headings of the organising bodies.

FITA (FEDERATION INTERNATIONALE DE TIR A L'ARC.)

FITA recognises only two classes, Barebow and Freestyle.

Barebow

The bow may not be a compound, must be bare and free from any protrusions, marks or blemishes or laminated pieces which could be of use in aiming. There may be no sights, draw-checks, clickers or mounted stabilisers. A sling may be used. Arrows may be made of any material. The top end of the serving of the string must not end within the archer's vision at full draw. It may have no attachments other than those to locate the nocking point. The finger-position and anchor-position on the face must not change during the shooting of a round. Judges will check and note the positions used during tackle inspection before an important tournament. If desired, three fingers may be placed under the arrow. Field glasses or binoculars may be used in shooting marked distances, but not on unmarked distances.

Freestyle

The bow may not be a compound, but may be fitted if desired with sights, adjustable arrow-plate, pressure button, clicker or draw-check and stabilisers up to the number of four with or without TFC's (an unused TFC remaining on the bow counts as a stabiliser). The top end of the string serving must not end within the archer's vision at full draw. The string may have an attachment not greater in diameter than 1 cm to serve as a lip or nose mark. Field glasses and binoculars may be used on marked distances, not on unmarked. For both classes, arrows must be marked with rings approximately 5 mm in width to indicate shaft number. All arrows in any target must be similar in fletching and length.

GNAS (GRAND NATIONAL ARCHERY SOCIETY)

GNAS recognises the FITA classes of Barebow and Freestyle. In addition GNAS recognises the following classes:

Traditional

In this class, archers shoot as barebow, but must use arrows with wooden shafts. They may, however, be fletched with feathers or plastic vanes, and may have plastic nocks. GNAS recognises a number of rounds apart from FITA Hunter and Field, and in these binoculars are not allowed at all. Organisers are at liberty to provide awards in classes for Longbow or for Compounds if they choose. Compound bow users may take part in GNAS rounds, but not to compete directly against users of the recurve or composite bows.

Juniors

There are classes in all GNAS rounds, including the FITA ones shot by GNAS, for juniors under 18, juniors under 15, and juniors under 12, with some shortening of distances for the latter two age-groups.

EFAA (ENGLISH FIELD ARCHERY ASSOCIATION)

Barebow

The regulations are similar to those of FITA except that stabilisers are permitted as long as they cannot be used for sighting aids, and an under-arrow draw-check is allowed. Both face-walking and string-walking are permitted, and so is the use of compounds.

Freestyle

Mechanical releases (except for the disabled) are not allowed, nor are sighting devices incorporating a lens or prism. Apart from that, almost any equipment is allowed, including compounds, peep sights and levelling devices.

Bowhunter (adults only)

In general the regulations are similar to FITA Barebow, except that in Bowhunter, the arrow *must* be located between 1st and 2nd fingers, and that bow quivers, brush buttons and silencers may be used. There is also permission to use stabilisers, provided they are not over 12″ in length, and a condition that field piles of at least a stated weight *must* be used. There is no face-walking, but compounds may be used.

Hunting Style

This is like Bowhunter, except that no stabilisers are allowed, and only wooden feather-fletched arrows may be used.

Longbow

There is a Longbow class.

Unlimited

The only difference between this and EFAA Freestyle is that release aids and telescopic sights may be used.

Juniors

As with GNAS, provision is made for juniors, where the upper age limit is the 17th birthday, and for 'cubs', with an upper age limit of 13th birthday. In EFAA binoculars may not be used by an archer before he has finished shooting all his arrows in any target. Nearly all EFAA shoots take place over marked distances.

The Scottish Field Archery Association (SFAA) and the Welsh Field Archery Association (WFAA) are organised on similar lines to the EFAA.

NFAS (NATIONAL FIELD ARCHERY SOCIETY)

All NFAS shoots are over courses with unmarked distances. No binoculars, range-finders or cameras are allowed.

Barebow

Similar to FITA and GNAS Barebow. For the hold, the index finger must touch the nock. Stabilisers may be used provided they do not exceed the archer's draw-length, and provided they cannot be used as a sight. No face-walking or string-walking is allowed.

Freestyle

There is almost complete freedom of choice of equipment, except that no release aids (except for the disabled) or compounds may be used.

Hunting Tackle

As for Barebow except that no external stabilisers are allowed; arrows must be of wood fletched with feathers; the 'Mediterranean' loose only is permitted.

Longbow

As for Barebow except that arrows must be of wood. There are controls regulating the purity of design of the long-bow.

Freestyle No Sights

The title is self-explanatory. Archers may use clicker, draw-checks of any type, attachments to the string, and stabilisers not exceeding the archer's draw-length. It is permitted to use face-walking and string-walking techniques.

Unlimited

This class shoots as freestyle, but compounds may be used with or without release aids.

Crossbows

Crossbows are permitted as a class, subject to safety controls of various kinds. Telescopic or magnifying sights are not permitted and the weapons must be shot 'off hand' without the aid of any rest or support.

Juniors

Juniors (ages 12 to 15 years inclusive) are given some concessions regarding distances.

6

RULES AND REGULATIONS

Already some of the regulations governing styles of shooting have necessarily been referred to in the chapter on classes and styles. To deal in detail with rules of shooting would be tedious and the information would very rapidly become out of date. Instead, I propose to look at a few of the rules that affect shooting to show their purpose and effectiveness (or lack of it!)

Rules fall into three classes: those which are designed to ensure safety, those which control competition and those which are intended to prevent cheating. In addition there are the unwritten rules, or the code of accepted practice, which might loosely be called etiquette.

SAFETY RULES

Safety regulations demand that signs are put up to warn walkers from departing from the right of way in the vicinity of a shoot, and that there are direction signs for the archers to follow the right route around a course. Sometimes this is done by direction arrows, by triangular pointers, or by coloured tapes attached to bushes and trees. A 'safe path' is sometimes arranged so as to allow working parties to bring replacement faces in safety, and to allow archers who finish early to leave the course without walking into danger from other archers who are still shooting.

In laying a course, organisers must ensure that overshots from one target cannot reach archers shooting at other targets or progressing between targets. Targets are not to be set on the top of a hill where a miss may become a lethal flight shot. If a target needs to be sited where a miss could conceivably cause danger, a back-stop could be used to render it safe, but in general such shots are to be avoided by course setters. A minimum distance apart for adjacent targets may be specified, so that archers shooting in parallel lanes do not put each other at risk. To lay a course so as to make it perfectly safe is not easy. Some organisations provide for inspection and chartering of suitable permanent courses, and safety is certainly one of their requirements.

Strict regulations control the times when archers may walk up to score and collect arrows. In general, it is a good practice for all archers to remain behind those who are shooting, but there is a temptation for those who have shot to stay forward in a presumedly 'safe' position to 'spot' stray arrows shot by those whose turn to shoot comes later. This is especially liable to happen when poor shots are included in the group. No one likes to waste time hunting for lost arrows belonging to someone else, or abandoning one of his own, quite apart from the embarrassment of holding up following groups. All the same, rules which prohibit 'spotters' are a sound safety precaution, for there is always the possibility of an arrow ricocheting off a tree and going in a quite unexpected direction.

Although not included in the rule books, it is common practice for a bow to be leant against a target face as an indication that archers are searching for lost arrows behind the target where they may not be observed.

COMPETITION RULES

Competition rules take up a large part of the rule books of any organisation. Archers often deplore the fact that there seem to be so many pettifogging rules to be observed and try to ignore them if they can get away with it, but in fact it is the archers themselves who cause the proliferation of rules by attempting to get round the plain intention of a rule in order to gain advantage over other archers. So more rules have to be introduced to ensure equal conditions for all. As the sport becomes more competitive, there will be more rules – that is unavoidable. What I would like to see are rules that are more explicit and more simply expressed. Furthermore, I do not think a rule should be made unless it can be implemented.

One of the rules which is hard to put into practice is the ban by

FITA on string-walking and face-walking. It is stated that the archer's draw position and the relationship of arrow to drawing fingers must not change. That's all very well and good, but it is very hard to control this, even by the use of Polaroid photographs or by plotting arrow position against the face at tackle inspection, and observing through binoculars during the shoot. I believe that it would be more logical to define what equipment may be used and leave the archer to use it in any way that he finds most effective for himself, as long as it is safe.

Most of the regulations are indeed concerned with distinguishing between what is allowed in the Freestyle or Unlimited classes and what is forbidden to the various types of Barebow classes – and here there is considerable variation between what is allowed by the different organisations. However, all organisations agree that no archer should be allowed the use of any apparatus that could be used to estimate distance in unmarked rounds, and that no archer may refer to notes or memoranda that might be a means of improving his score. That sounds straightforward, but there are snags in enforcing these rules. The freestyle archer uses a sight; that sight may be an aperture sight. A skilful archer may know the amount of target area that that sight covers at a given distance and estimate accordingly. True, the judges may rule that having set his sight and presented the sight to the target, he may not alter it on that shot, even if he comes down and decides to draw up again. But they cannot prevent him from aiming high or low to compensate.

We can take as another example the question of sight tracks. These may be calibrated in inches or centimetres on the track. The archer needs to refer to a conversion chart for setting the sight for given distances. He is allowed to use such a marking guide, but he is not allowed to refer to data regarding the distances between which the various size faces are to be set in the Hunter round shot unmarked, for these give at least some clue to distances and could be a means of improving score. It is easy to see how this other information could be included on a card, or in a score book, or even codified. An archer is not allowed to have a sight track calibrated for a particular permanent course, for here modifications to allow for angles of slope could figure.

Barebow archers are not allowed a sight, or anything that could serve as a sight, like an over-arrow clicker, a poker in a certain position, or laminations or blemishes on the bow above the bow-hand. Yet the archer must use an arrow, and the arrow can be used for deliberate aiming as well as being shot 'instinctively'. 'Method shooters' employ the pile as a means of measuring the gap, and the shaft for alignment. This cannot be stopped, even if one wished to do so. Again, some take-down bows have locking-nuts, etc, which hold the bow together. These can be used as a guide to aiming, as can the upper edge of the sight window to frame the target at comparatively short ranges with an under-chin anchor.

A barebow archer might attempt to string-walk or face-walk although the rules of his organisation do not allow it. Here it is up to the other archers in his group to protest and appeal to the judges. At the same time, the TC will have recorded or noted his normal shooting anchor-point and finger-hold, perhaps using a chart such as that shown in Figure 8: *A* means that the arrow is located *above* the three fingers; *B* means that it is located *between* the first two fingers; the numbered positions are those that the arrow might assume at draw – after all, it is the position of the arrow relative to the eye that is the significant factor. A patch stuck on the bow by the TC will record the position the archer has chosen to use. Since this record is apparent to other archers (and to the TC who might be watching through binoculars) the archer is not likely to deviate from it.

No matter what the regulation, some archers will find ways of circumventing it. To ensure fair opportunity for all, however, there are rules about alternating the order of shooting, so that at some point each archer gets a clear target to shoot at. There are other rules that oblige course setters to ensure that each of a pair of posts provides a shot of equal difficulty. To ensure that archers are using legitimate equipment a tackle inspection is held before an important shoot, and arrows are checked to see that they are named or marked in such a way that no dispute can arise over ownership.

Other regulations control the different rounds, the distances of the shots, the dimensions of the faces and the scoring values.

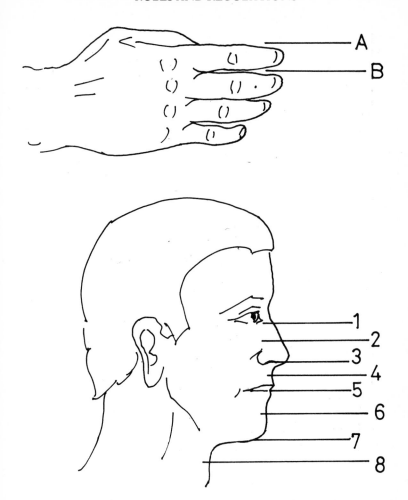

FIGURE 8   Face and finger positions

These would be tedious to relate and such information will be included in the rule books of the various organisations. There are many different rounds: Hunter's, Standard Field, Forester's, Big Game, British Wild Life, Swedish Big Game, Safari, Poachers, to name but a selection.

One principal difference in scoring concepts is revealed by score values. One may have roundels scoring various points values according to the distance of the ring from the centre, as 5, 4, 3 in FITA Hunter and Field, or 15, 10, 5 in Forester's. On the other hand, an animal face may have scores which are affected by whether the scoring arrow is shot 1st, 2nd or 3rd shot, and whether it is in a 'kill' area (heart and lungs) or 'wound' area (balance of animal, excluding superficial features). Some scoring values are in the Big Game class as follows: kill on first arrow=20 points, wound on 2nd arrow=10 points, kill on 3rd arrow=8 points. The difference is largely bound up with the degree of involvement the organisation has with either target archery or hunting.

A point which must be borne in mind is that some rounds are designed for the pleasure of shooting, or for a competition on a sole occasion, whereas others are used for comparison and team selections. The latter must therefore be standardised to some extent. The Standard Field round is what its name indicates; wherever shot, the distances and sizes of faces are always the same. True, there is a variation of terrain and conditions, but apart from that, one Standard round score can be justly compared with another and record scores be made and broken. The FITA Hunter round is subject to a degree of standardisation, too, even though distances are not usually marked. This is ingeniously arranged by ensuring that each size of face must be set within certain overall limits of distance, but that the distances of all the shots taken at each size of face come to an agreed total. Thus, the twelve shots taken at the three 60 cm faces in a unit must total 480 metres, and the distance of all the 56 shots in one unit must total 1480 metres (2 units of 14 targets each, equal one round). So again, some degree of comparison of one FITA Hunter round with another is possible. The planning and laying of such a course is a bit of a headache for course setters, though; in comparison, the Standard Field round is child's play to lay out. Still, the fact that the actual individual distances of the Hunter's round are not disclosed and that every shot is from a different post is a great attraction, so it is a popular round. The scoring being in circular zones puts a premium on accurate shooting.

So far I have not said anything about time control. This is a vexed question, for some archers, especially those using hunting or traditional styles, or indeed most barebow styles, shoot quickly and are 'thrown' out of their normal rhythm by competing in the same groups as freestylers who in general take longer. Sometimes, indeed, it is possible to put barebow and freestyle archers in different groups, but this is not always convenient. Even then, unless the different stylists are accommodated on different courses, there is still the likelihood of the barebow groups catching up the freestyle groups, however carefully the organiser or field captain allocates the targets on which the groups start, to allow for this.

Time control has long been established in target archery, where 'traffic lights' and other systems can be employed to control shooting on a regimental basis, but such an idea is not feasible in field archery. Nevertheless, in the mid 1970s, delays caused principally by freestylers with clicker trouble caused frustration among other archers and there were even occasions when tournaments continued as dusk fell. Accordingly, FITA made a rule that a time limit of 1½ minutes per arrow (note, 1½ minutes per arrow, not 6 minutes for 4 arrows) shall be allowed, from the time the archer takes his position at the post, this time limit to be enforced at the direction of the TC (Technical Commission), and the archer to be warned by the TC before the time limit is enforced. Although 1½ minutes is a long time (even in target archery, a limit of 2½ minutes is allowed for 3 arrows) this does prevent unreasonably slow shooters from holding up a tournament, while permitting an archer to exceed the limit at least once if he should get into some sort of trouble. There is one loophole and that is the phrase 'from the time the archer takes his position at the post'. An archer might deliberately hang back and observe the target faces at length before going to his post, but the TC and other competitors should tell him in no uncertain terms that this is not permitted. Again, when you are estimating distance, to stand, say, 5 metres behind the posts will not enable you to make a true estimate. One needs to be standing at the post to get an accurate picture.

In Britain, at any rate, consideration is given to junior participants, even below the age of 12, and recognition made of the lower poundage of their bows by allowing them to shoot at closer distances. If the round is marked, there is no problem in setting forward junior posts. But if the round is unmarked, then one has to be careful to give no clue as to distance to the archers who are yet to shoot the full distances. At one time the FITA Hunter round shot to GNAS rules allowed for under 15's to shoot from the front post at 60 cm faces, but not at the 45 cm faces. This didn't work fairly, because either no indication was given to the juniors which size faces were which, in which case they could lose the value of their scores if shot wrongly, or an indication could be given, in which case the older archers would thereby know which faces were which and estimate accordingly. The present system is much fairer – the junior aged 12 to 14 shoots two arrows from each of the front two posts wherever one face only is exposed (this means it is either 45 cm or 60 cm, but you don't know which). On target butts where a pattern of faces appear, this age-group shoots from all the posts, as adults do. In other rounds similar concessions are made by GNAS. Other organisations, likewise, arrange for junior posts to be used in such a way that no information is given to adult archers that they should not have. It is often recommended that juniors shoot last, so that the number of steps they take to reach their forward posts cannot be a source of information to the archers who have to shoot after them.

In the early days of field archery, shooting skills were less developed. Consequently one target face was usually deemed sufficient, even a small face at short range, but with increasing skill and greater concentration of arrows, it became necessary to set up multiple faces to avoid unreasonable damage to arrows and loss of points by deflections. Next, regulations regarding the order of shooting the faces had to be introduced, and then the arrows had to be shot in a specified order and and be numbered, so that a bad arrow in the wrong target face could not be claimed as a good arrow in the right one.

PREVENTION OF CHEATING

I have now reached the narrow borderline between keeping to

the rules of competition and deliberate malpractice. Obviously one must attempt to prevent actual falsification of scores. The best regulation here is the appointment of two archers out of each group of four to act as scorers with a score card each, which must be kept independently and scores cross-checked before the arrows are withdrawn. If in spite of this, cards are returned which show discrepancies, the lower score is the one that is accepted. Each group of archers may also have a captain, whose task is to control shooting in his group and resolve disputes, and give a first decision on doubtful scores, subject to an appeal to a member of the TC (if one can be found when required). At FITA World Championships independent non-shooting scorers are provided.

In spite of all this it is still possible for cheating to take place; if it does, it is because all the archers in the group are being negligent in observing the rules. If the rules are kept to, cheating is virtually impossible. I would not wish to suggest that cheating is anything but very rare in archery, but as in any other competitive sport it is a possibility and the rules must take cognizance of this. Furthermore, even the suspicion that someone might be cheating should be prevented as far as possible, so as to ensure harmony and a happy atmosphere.

Most attempted infractions of the rules relate to the desire to find out the unmarked distances. For this reason, archers are not allowed formally to pace the distances between posts, or to use any form of distance-measuring aid, or to disclose to other archers what they think the distance is, or 'spot' for others and tell them where the arrows strike and so on.

The sets of multiple faces, as I have said already, necessitate arrow numbering, for an arrow shot at target face 1 could fall in, say, face 2, and be ignored in all honesty by the archer, who would discount it as a miss and not bother to observe exactly where it landed. If later he put another arrow in face 2 correctly shot, falling alongside the former arrow, but scoring fewer points, there would be a great temptation to persuade himself that the high scoring arrow was the one correctly shot. Accordingly, arrows shot at multiple faces in FITA rounds must be shot in ascending numerical order and be ring-marked clearly with

5 mm bands. The reason for the prominent band-marking is to ensure that the other archers on the target can *see* what arrows the archer is claiming however they may lie in the target. Otherwise it might be necessary to touch the arrows to twist them so as to see where the numbering was, so giving an opportunity (or an accidental chance) of altering the lie of an arrow near the line between two scoring zones. The reasoning behind this is therefore quite logical, and rarely understood by many archers who resist putting bands on their arrows. Of course, if adhesive coloured plastic tape of the right dimensions is used, it can easily be removed for a target shoot, or one arrow's number altered if owing to loss or damage the archer during a field shoot needs to produce another no 2 arrow; in this case he could peel off a band or two from a higher value spare arrow before shooting what would become a no 2 arrow. The same need to recognise arrows in the face without touching them is even more evident in the Big Game and other animal rounds, because there is such a high points difference between 1st arrow hits and 2nd and 3rd arrow hits. At long distances (without, of course, binoculars which are not allowed) it is not possible to see where an arrow strikes, and as I have said, spotters are not allowed by most organisations.

ETIQUETTE

Lastly, though not written of in most rule books, there is a code of practice whereby archers are encouraged to behave responsibly and not attempt to disconcert fellow competitors.

In competition it is not thought courteous to insist on taking the most favourable of pairs of posts all day, or to take, say, the left-hand posts all day if you happen to like shooting from that side. Instead, it is customary to change posts after 14 targets of a 28 target round. It is not fair play to stand on the 1st post of a walk-up spending extra time observing the distance, while previous archers are still shooting from the remaining posts. If a judge were there he could well point out that the archer who does this is using up his quota of time and penalise him if he takes too long later in making his shot, but judges can only be in one place at a time.

One should not remove obstructions such as twigs or branches once a shoot has begun and other archers have suffered the inconvenience. There could be a case for removing obstructions that have occurred *during* the shoot, such as branches having been weighed down by rain, but in such a case the archers should appeal to the TC to attend to the hazard. Even where a shot has been incorrectly laid, it must remain incorrect for the remainder of the shoot. For this reason, archers on arriving at their first target should study it carefully, and in the case of any doubt, should call the TC, in the interests of themselves and of those who are to follow them.

Obviously, distracting other archers' attention while they are shooting is to be deplored. Most archers, however, are very considerate of each other, and if they do transgress the rules it is more often out of a desire to be friendly and help others than to do them down. But, of course, you help beginners best by making them aware of the rules, seeing that they keep to them – and letting them see that you do, too.

7

IMPROVING THE SCORE

Once an archer has joined a club, learnt to handle the bow, found a style that suits him, taken part in a number of field shoots, and started to absorb the thoughts and ideas that archers everywhere are eager to share with each other, he may fairly call himself a field archer, but he is a long way from achieving his full potential. The object of this chapter is to outline (it can do no more) a few of the areas in which he might seek improvement independently or with the aid of a coach or fellow archers.

Briefly then, he can improve the following things: his tackle, his technique, his fitness – and he can examine his approach to the sport so that he can see exactly what he wants to get out of it. None of these points will be of much avail without the others; it is best to aim for improvement on all fronts.

TACKLE

It does not follow that the most expensive tackle is necessarily the best, though the tendency will be that way. Expensive tackle that is not suited to the archer is useless, or worse than useless. We have seen newcomers to the sport rapidly acquire all the most advanced equipment and, let us be honest, gimmicks, too, which they see top-class performers using, only to find their scores are little better than before, and in disillusionment they pack it in and dispose of their expensive equipment cheaply.

You can experiment quite legitimately with the use of stabiliser systems, clickers, or sizes and designs of sight apertures, where allowed, as in all freestyle classes. In barebow or freestyle a different shape of handle-grip (often alternatives are offered) or a different length of handle-riser could be advantageous.

Carbon-fibre limbs or Kevlar strings can improve an archer's score if used properly. In all cases, you should not be hasty, but gather all available advice before making a decision – better still, if you can, try out borrowed items before committing yourself to an expense that could prove valueless.

The important things about tackle are matching and tuning.

Matching

Matching need not detain us long, since aspects of the subject have been covered in other chapters. There is the matching of arrows to bow to consider, where manufacturers' recommendations are a good guide, but remember that a high-performance bow of a given draw-weight may well require different arrow specifications from those required by a bow of lower performance (slower cast, in fact). The size and height of fletching must suit the arrows, and the archer's style, and the nature of the courses he chooses to shoot over should be taken into account. Then there is the suitability of the bow to the archer, a kind of matching if you like. A bow designed to be used at 28″ (71 cm) or thereabouts will not perform well at 25″ (63 cm) – the charts cannot allow for such variables. All the same, by experimenting, a set of arrows will be found that will shoot satisfactorily. The archer would do better to dispose of an unsuitable bow as soon as he realises its deficiencies and start afresh. This is why I recommend getting good advice *before* purchasing your first bow, so as to avoid disappointment.

Matched arrows are essential (that is, arrows that are matched not only to the bow, but to each other). All reputable sets of arrows are matched to some extent. Get the best matching you can afford, for controlled materials, straightness, length, weight, fletching, shaft-size and spine. There are enough variables to meet without those introduced by inferior arrows.

Tuning

A bow is said to be in tune, as an engine is, when it is adjusted to give the best performance it is capable of. A bow cannot adequately be tuned for you by someone else – you must do it for yourself, under guidance, if necessary. You must proceed in an orderly fashion, adjusting one thing at a time. The tackle should be set up with all attachments, such as stabilisers, exactly as it will be shot. Any changes to the basic set-up will necessitate starting the tuning process all over again. You should also have a consistent shooting style, or conclusions will be misleading: it is not an exercise for the beginner to attempt alone. I will deal only with the tuning of composite recurve bows. The tuning of compound bows involves other mechanical factors and adjustments which each manufacturer explains in terms of his own product.

Make sure your arrows are really straight, with nocks set straight to the shaft and uniformly to the fletchings, and fletchings that are set at precisely the same angle and spacing on each arrow. Nocks must be of exactly the same slot size. The string on the bow should be initially of the number of strands reckoned suitable by manufacturers and allow for bracing at a recommended height without undue twisting.

It is possible, indeed highly recommended, to use bare shafts in tuning. For ultra refinement, insulating tape can be wound on the shafts in the fletching area so as to compensate for the weight of the missing fletchings. The idea of using bare shafts is to eliminate the 'forgiving' effect of the fletchings which perform their intended function of steering the shaft on course. Faulty arrow performance is exaggerated by using bare shafts. On the other hand, normal-sized fletchings are not able to make much difference to arrow flight in the first few feet of flight. So we shall use fletched shafts in this exercise.

Set up the tackle, brace the bow, nock an arrow on the string, let it lie on the rest while you lean the bow against some convenient support that will allow you to retire a few feet to see if the arrow is lying more or less on the centre-line of the bow. If you have an adjustable pressure plate, adjust it so that the arrow points slightly to the left (for a right-hander). If you haven't, leave the set-up alone for the time being. What we are going to do is to try to get the arrows coming *straight* out of the bow with as little as possible of the 'snaking' effect at one time called 'the archer's paradox'. Since bows are now mostly cut past centre, this effect can be drastically reduced; there is no *need* for the arrow to curve around the bow-handle at the arrow-pass to fly true to the target. It *will* bend a little owing to the fact that the string slides round the loosing fingers on loose and proceeds in a wave-like motion to the point at which it releases the arrow, but we want this bending kept to a minimum.

Provide yourself with a target either of stramit or straw, set vertically at eye-level, but secured against falling over. Put an aiming mark on the target at about chin-height, and set sights, if you use any, at shortest possible range. Stand off, say, six feet (ie far enough for the arrow to clear the bow when shot into the target). Get a helper to tell you whether to aim up or down to present a truly horizontal shaft to the target. He may take a sighting on window ledges of a distant building, for example. Whether you are barebow or freestyle, adjust your aiming mark accordingly. Now all is ready, aim and loose. Shoot one arrow several times, to make sure you are shooting consistently. If the arrow goes in tails up your nocking point is too high and must be lowered. If it goes in tails down, it is too low and must be raised. Alter nocking-point by very small degrees until the arrow goes in level, then secure nocking-point.

Now we have reduced the vertical oscillation to a minimum, we will do the same to the horizontal oscillation. Set a series of six marks vertically down the target about four inches apart. Leave the sight at point-blank range. Shoot the first arrow at the top mark, move away about a yard and a half and shoot at the second mark, with the same sight setting. Carry on down. Now you will have six arrows in the target. Owing to the wave-like movement of the arrow as it leaves the bow, the shafts will not be parallel, but you will have gained a lot of information. If the angles are widely divergent, the arrow is flexing wildly; it may be too whippy, but more likely our later adjustments will cause it to fly steadily.

If the arrows in general go in tails right (for a right-hander) the arrow is not bending enough, but you could either soften the spring of a plunger-button or move the arrow-plate in. If neither of these adjustments are practicable, you could attempt the following:

1   try whippier arrows

2   reduce the bracing height a little, but not beyond a safe limit

3   use heavier piles

All these suggestions will make the arrow bend more while being shot.

If the arrows in general go in tails left (for a right-hander) the arrow is bending too much, but you could stiffen the spring of a plunger-button or move the arrow-plate out. If you have no arrow-plate, you could pack out the rest. Alternatively, you could:

1   try stiffer arrows

2   increase the bracing height modestly

3   use more strands in the string

All these suggestions will make the arrow bend less while being shot. The listed alternatives 1, 2, and 3 do involve other considerations than bow-tuning and may be disadvantageous in other ways. By repeated tests and adjustments you should arrive at a sweet shooting bow by which the arrows are delivered in as straight an initial flight path as possible. Try the bow, now, at all distances.

Other Factors

You may have problems caused by the fletchings, especially hard plastics, striking the riser on the belly, or face side as they pass. The arrows will be diverted to the right (for a right-hander). To detect this, put lipstick or wax marker on the edge of the suspect vanes and see if they mark the bow. If they do, you may have to use a lower profile vane, or try flexible vanes.

If you require an extreme sight adjustment to shoot the arrows centrally, the trouble is probably that your technique, and head, eye and hand position are at fault, rather than the arrows (if they are reasonably suited to the bow). If the bow is noisy, you may have the string too long so that bracing-height is too low, or the string may be too thin and 'elastic'. If the bow is braced too high, or if the string is too thick, it will not normally be too noisy, but you will lose cast. By the way, in trying different bracing-heights, you may need different string-lengths. Putting too many twists in a string affects its behaviour; 1½ turns per inch is a maximum.

The ideal is to make the best compromise you can; when the bow sounds sweet, feels sweet, and shoots sweet, it will be in tune.

TECHNIQUE

Grouping

The essential of technique is to get tighter groups. This involves precision in aiming of course, to some extent, but in far greater measure, precision in making the shot. If all arrows went where they were aimed, many archers' scores would improve dramatically. What happens all too often is that the arrow was aimed properly, but shot badly. Consistency is the essential feature to concentrate upon; not only should you *see* the shot is aimed properly, but *feel* it is shot properly. You should feel whether it is about to be shot properly or not, and if not, be prepared to come down and start again.

Freestylers and barebow method-shooters can study their patterns of shooting by recording on separate small target faces drawn (or printed) in a notebook, where each arrow struck. Recording may be by arrow number in order to check the equipment, of course; what I am suggesting you do here is to record the shots in order of shooting, thus, first arrow shot, second arrow shot, and so on. You may well find out that there is a tendency for all the first shots to go in one general area, and all the second shots to go off into another area, especially noticeable if you plot all first shots on one memo-sized target face, and all second shots on another, and so on.

Blindfold Study

If a definite pattern emerges, you can then investigate the possible causes. You may find that the arrow pattern moves progressively to the right or left. If so, draw up, aim, shut both eyes, hold on aim for as long as you can hold reasonably steady, and open the eyes again. If you have drifted off aim, it would suggest that your accustomed stance is not matched to your natural physical posture, and you should adjust it accordingly. You see, with your eyes open and aiming on a mark, you consciously maintain an aim even though sets of muscles are being brought into increasing stress to resist a natural tendency to drift off. The shot when made, is then performed less efficiently than a 'natural' shot.

By the blindfold exercise you may find faults in the vertical aim, also. Again, an observer may be able to tell you whether you 'creep' or not, if you do not thread the arrow through the clicker, or don't use one at all anyway. Once a variable has been identified you are part way towards effecting a cure.

Back-tension and the Loose

Most variables occur in the loose, the hardest part of the technique to perfect. This is closely connected with 'back tension', the term given to the control of the draw and hold, by correct maintenance of power in the back muscles. If all unnecessary effort is removed from the muscles in the arms and chest, a good loose will result when the bow is shot, for the drawing hand and loosing hand will fly apart without restriction. The loosing hand will fly back smoothly to a natural finishing position behind the neck or ear (according to the position of the original anchor-point) and in line with the draw-force line *prior* to the loose. This should ensure uniformity of shot.

The archer with an under-chin anchor can slightly increase pressure of the string on the chin just prior to the loose and assist this desirable effect; the archer with a cheek-anchor cannot do this, but he can still strive for good back-tension of balanced effort and get an equally good loose. The bow hand should break away to the left (for a right-hander) or stay presented to the target; it should not go to the right, for this will indicate tension in the bicep and chest muscles that could well be reduced.

An observer can tell you what you are doing. It is even better if you can see it for yourself by means of video in slow-motion, by cine-film shown at 3 frames per second or slower, or polaroid or other still photographs taken at the significant moment – if the cameraman can catch it! The archer's position just after the loose is often very revealing. One would hope to see the hands sprung apart and the back muscles closed fully. If the bow hand has moved across the chest, and the loosing hand is still by the face, or worse, flung sideways from the face, a consistent loose is unlikely to be achieved on consecutive shots.

Each Shot a New Shot

Archery involves a series of repetitive exercises, to some extent rendered less repetitive in field archery by the changing nature of the terrain, and by the variation in distances and direction of shot. All the same, an attempt must be made to ensure uniformity of procedure in every other way, especially after having addressed the target. A standard routine should be adhered to wherever possible. The 'instinctive' archer may object that he shoots better when he does not deliberate too much. Yes, of course, that is quite true, but I am saying that he should clear his mind for each shot in the same way.

This brings us to the four shots from one post problem. Many instinctive archers do better on first or second shot than on third or fourth, the reason being that an undesirable awareness of previous shots obstructs the natural feel of the required shot. The advice here is to put out of the mind the previous shot and look away from the target for a short time, before addressing it again. If the archer were allowed to walk off the post and come back to it for each shot it would make it easier to treat each shot as a fresh shot, but he is not allowed to do this. The freestyler or method-shooter should profit by observing the fate of previous shots, but still not let himself get up-tight over what happened to those shots, whether they were good or bad; having made his decision regarding aiming, etc, he should begin the routine of making the shot with a mind unclouded by either self-congratulation or anxiety.

Distance Judging

Accurate judgement of distance is essential for shooting unmarked rounds. If the first shot is not at least on the target, you have no information to assist you in making the next shot, and if you are not scoring well with the first shots you will not make the really high scores. For this, there is nothing like regular practice, seeing targets in different light conditions and over dead ground. If there is a drop in the ground between you and the target, you may not allow for the space you cannot see, and think the target is closer than it is. If there is an excess of area apparent to the eye below eye-level, as for instance over a sheet of water, the target will appear to be further away than it really is. It is of great assistance, of course, firstly to know by heart the distances between which the various size faces may be set, and secondly to be able to distinguish between the various sizes of face, either by hard-gained skill, or by memorising the animal figure displayed, if it is that sort of target face.

Apart from actually looking at targets on a course, you can also improve your ability to judge distance by making a habit of doing so all day long while about your ordinary affairs, judging the distance to a lamp-post or a parked vehicle for example, and verifying your opinion by pacing it out.

But no matter how skilful you become, you will sometimes be deceived by a cunningly set target, so make sure your arrows are fletched and nocked in colours which are easily visible at a distance, so that you can see where that first arrow goes. After that, you should be able to make the necessary adjustment of posture, gap, or sight.

Knowing the Performance of the Bow

Sight users would do well to go out on a flat field and deliberately shoot at variable distances on the same sight setting to see, for instance, just how high an arrow flies when shot 2 metres or 2 yards short at an intended 30 metres or yards, and at an intended 40, and so on. Then experiment to see how much difference 2 or 3 metres or yards over length makes at each of the likely distances. Armed with this knowledge, an archer who is an accurate shot has only to get an arrow on the target somewhere to ensure that the rest are in or near the spot or top scoring zone.

The Regular Gap

One slight advantage the gap-shooter has in the matter of distance judging is related to the angular variation of the same gap seen at different distances. For example he may find that with this particular finger position, anchor-point and cast of bow that he

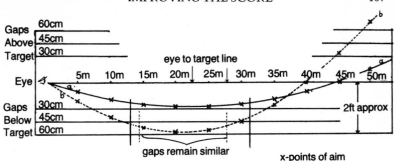

FIGURE 9   Comparing the gaps

can aim 1 foot below the spot at any distance from 15 to 40 metres. This is because the closer he gets to the target, the bigger the deflection of aim that same gap provides. The more powerful the bow, the longer the distance will be where precise distance calculation is not critical. If you have a bow with an absolutely flat trajectory (which is impossible) you would have the same gap at *all* distances, or no gap at all at *any* distances if the arrow were drawn to eye-level. But with any bow there is bound to be a series of ranges where there will be an automatic compensation between gap (as measured and seen at target distance) and distance between the archer and target. A diagram may make this clearer; see Figure 9.

SLOPE WORK

You will probably find that as your experience of field archery grows, it will become easier to adjust your technique to differing degrees of slope. Also, you will learn how to judge the effect of slopes on the arrow in flight. See Plates 11 and 12. The arrow, like any other projectile, flies in a parabola. Gravity exerts its greatest effect on the arrow in horizontal flight in pulling it away from the direction it was originally shot in, affecting it at right-angles to its flight path. If the arrow were shot vertically upward, it would not diverge from its original flight path, but would eventually stop, fall backward, turn over and descend. If it were shot vertically downwards it would travel straight and continue on the same path until it eventually hit something. So if the arrow is shot upwards at a steep angle or downwards at a steep

Plate 11a
Shooting the slopes

Plate 11b

Plate 12

The aim and the shot

angle, the parabola will be flattened, because gravity will not be pulling at right-angles to the line of flight (see Figure 10).

This means that at very steep angles up or down, the archer has to be prepared to take off distance. One would expect to take off distance downhill; it is a little surprising to have to take off distance uphill, but this is so. The arrow is affected by gravity immediately it leaves the bow, but for the first part of its flight, this has little noticeable effect. Very roughly, we can say that an arrow flies flattish for the earlier part of its flight, and on an ever-steepening curve for the latter part.

So, it may be concluded and it has been verified in practice,

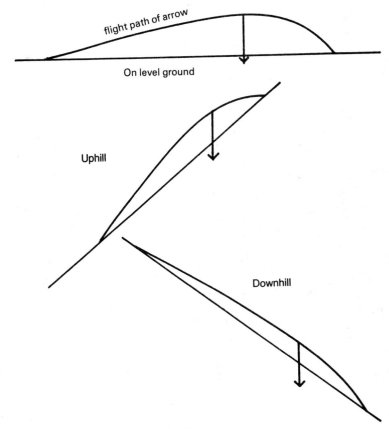

FIGURE 10   Direction of gravitational pull

that arrows may be shot at normal marks whatever the slope, within reason, up to a given distance. This distance will vary according to the power of the bow, the weight of the arrows, etc, and also according to the severity of the slope. After that point the effect of the slope will become more and more apparent. There will be a different cut-off point for uphill than for down-hill.

Nevertheless, the following may be said to be true:

1   On shallow slopes, there will be little or no effect, except maybe at the longest ranges.
2   On very steep slopes downhill, one will need to aim low quite a bit, even at comparatively short ranges.
3   On very steep slopes uphill, one will probably need to aim a little low at the longer distances. At very long ranges, longer than 60 metres, there will eventually come a point where one has to aim high, but that is not likely to occur below 60 metres at 45 degrees, except with a light bow or very heavy arrows.

So much for up and down the slopes. Now what about across the slopes, that is, along the contours.

Contrary to popular belief, there is no physical reason why a correctly shot arrow should drift downhill, yet we know that arrows appear to have a tendency to do this. The reason is that they are often not correctly shot. Factors which cause you to lean from the vertical or to cant the bow are as follows:

1   The slope on which you are standing
2   The slope on which the target is placed
3   Visible lines of slope between you and the target
4   Distant background effects

There is a tendency in everyone to lean into the slope as a natural precaution against falling off. The bow follows this cant, with the result that the arrow is actually directed down the slope. Sight users are obviously more vulnerable than barebow archers because the sight needs to be kept vertically above the arrow for accurate aim.

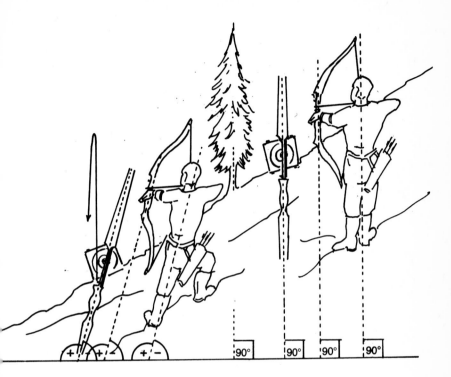

FIGURE 11   Keeping upright

So remember, resist the temptation to lean too far into the slope. Make sure you are really standing vertically and that your bow is upright, too (if that is the way you usually shoot it!) Look out for clues to assist you in preserving an upright posture, such as verticals on buildings, or trees that happen to grow straight up (some do, some don't). If this is properly done, the arrows will not drift down the slope (see Figure 11). With diagonal shots there will be two factors to consider: remember that the actual slope of the shot will be less than if it was shot straight up and down (which is obvious), and that the effect of slope on the eye will be just as disconcerting as the condition described in shooting along the contours. So, consider how severe the slope actually is, preserve an upright body position and don't tilt the bow (unless you always shoot with a canted bow).

ASSESSING THE CONDITIONS

One way in which the experienced archer scores over the novice is in observing the weather. Before setting out on a course, he will decide what equipment he will need to take with him for warmth or for keeping dry, for instance. He will not be without insect-repellent in conditions where the pests may be a nuisance, or without sunburn lotion on scorching hot days. In fact, he will take every precaution to avoid physical discomfort impairing his shooting.

Then again, you need to know the effect of light and shade on your judgement of distance; targets that are brightly lit up appear to be closer than they really are, and darker ones appear more distant. As you proceed round a course, you need to be prepared for shooting directly into the sun, which can be very difficult, especially uphill. Something to use as a visor, like a peaked cap, or dark glasses, is a great help.

The question of slopes has already been studied, but the effect of the wind needs to be allowed for, also, by adjusting the sight or by aiming off. The effect of cross-winds are obvious, but head or following winds are more tricky. At a relatively short distance a head wind may cause an arrow to lift a little and go high, especially uphill, whereas at longer distances it will be slowed down and drop low. The skilled archer knows by experience how much adjustment or aim-off to allow – there is no other way of learning it. The target archer has trouble with wind often enough, but he is at any rate shooting consistently in the same direction, and may have flags on the tops of the targets to inform him of wind direction and strength, but the field archer will have to cope with the wind coming from all directions as he shoots round a course. He will probably meet more variable winds, too, because of the broken ground he is using. He is less likely to be as exposed as the target archer though, and the distances are shorter in field archery, which is some consolation.

Lastly, an old hand is always alert and watches closely the shots of the other archers in his group for information that may help him. And not only does he watch, he listens too – there is a perceptibly longer duration between loose and impact of an arrow shot at 50 metres and one shot at 40 metres, for example.

FITNESS

How far you go in this direction depends on how dedicated you are to field archery; whether you view it as a competitive sport or whether you follow it as a recreation. Admittedly, archery is not a sport where supreme physical fitness would appear to be vital. But this is an argument in favour of some training, for unlike, say, swimming, rugby or cycling, the actual participation in archery does not of itself markedly improve the physique or the capacity to become fitter for the sport. Of course, there is the question of what fitness really is. If you undertake any exercises, it will be to improve fitness for archery, not necessarily fitness in terms of other sports.

Considering the nature of archery, you will find you require no excess weight to heave up and down slopes, nor should you be seriously underweight which will mean less resistance to cold weather and to the strain of shooting all day with little opportunity for food or rest. Without making a fetish of it you should endeavour to get your weight to a level appropriate to your build and body type. To reduce your weight may mean self-control at first, and maybe a 'crash' diet for not more than three days at a time to accustom the stomach to taking less food. Once your weight reaches the desired level, it is not too difficult to maintain it, provided you eat recommended food sensibly.

Another requirement of field archery is a steady pulse-rate, and quick recovery after exertion, so that the shot can be made under control even after a steep climb. A good cardio-vascular respiratory (CVR) response is required also for rapid replenishment of nutriment to the muscles via the blood-stream, as well as to improve the exchange of oxygen and carbon dioxide in the lungs. The best exercise for this is probably jogging – trotting at a pace that does not cause one to pant, but only to breathe deeply. Even in cities there are parks or less frequented ways that may be used for this purpose, and if all else fails, you can run on the spot indoors. The hard part of any formal physical programme is to follow it regularly even when you are not inclined to turn out, or have become bored with it. To avoid boredom, vary the route, or go with a companion, or vary the pace between walking, sprinting for short bursts and steady jogging. Of course, if you have the slightest doubt about your heart condition you should consult your doctor before undertaking running exercises, but if you are normally fit, in most cases he will thoroughly approve the idea, for more people suffer from heart ailments through lack of exercise than through over-vigorous exertion. As another means of avoiding boredom, introduce a measurement to show you how you improve. Compare your normal pulse-rate with what it is immediately after a jogging session, and then again one minute after you have stopped. You should find an increasingly rapid rate of recovery.

Exercises with springs can be very helpful. Some springs like the Bullworker have the facility for compression as well as extension, and for the provision of a scale on which to measure your rate of improvement. Isometric exercises are good, in that they require only short periods of static tension, for it is not easy to find time for exercise in addition to a busy life. But isometric exercises involve sets of muscles only at one point in their movement, and furthermore do not provide CVR exercise, so in addition you should undertake jogging or some similar pursuit.

Weight-training – not weight-lifting – is beneficial, in that less heavy weights are used in repetition exercises, so that you can gradually increase muscle power without undue strain. It is best to restrict weight-training to no more than two sessions a week, in order to allow the muscles to 'grow' after the periods of exercise. You might think erroneously that only the main muscles of the arms and back need strengthening. This is a grave mistake; a great many other muscles are involved in drawing the bow and loosing it efficiently, not least those that maintain the posture, so don't restrict exercise to arms alone.

Turning to oriental systems of exercise, the practice of Hatha Yoga is to be recommended, because it increases breath control, suppleness, mental discipline and concentration – all absolutely vital in archery. There is no need to get involved in the spiritual and meditative aspects unless you wish, nor with the more intricate exercises – it is enough to practise regular breathing by good diaphragm control, some of the simple exercises such as the Sun exercise, and total relaxation, which can in turn lead to more beneficial sleep. It is even said that the yoga student will find his weight regularise itself whatever he eats, but perhaps it is more likely that he eats more advisedly.

Regarding tobacco and alcohol, I have little to say beyond stating as a fact that they do you no good at all. But the reader who indulges modestly is not likely to be prepared to give them up for the sake of his archery, unless he's a fanatic. There are so many other things that aren't good for us, such as refined sugar, polished rice, or a cholesterol-saturated diet, that you have to keep a sense of proportion. By way of preparation for a tournament, you should endeavour to continue eating, drinking, smoking, sleeping and so on as you normally do. An early night will do no good if you are not accustomed to retire early, as you will only lie awake. Deciding to give up smoking for the duration of an event is likely to lead to irritability. Food and drink could be kept as normal, though there is some point in increasing the protein intake shortly before an event, and in taking glucose in liquid or tablet form to give 'instant' energy not only to the muscles but also to the brain. Lastly, your physical fitness will be of little avail unless your mental fitness is equally well-developed. So make sure that all your tackle is in perfect order, with all necessary spares shot in and ready for use, and leave yourself plenty of time for travel. Haste and anxiety can undo all the good work of training and preparation.

ATTITUDE TO THE SPORT

This can be stated very briefly – the ideal is to *think positively*; but this bald statement needs clarifying.

Take the example of the archer who after a few wild shots goes utterly to pieces and withdraws from the shoot. He was very likely thinking negatively; instead of saying 'What do I do to regain good form?' he thinks 'I wonder what's gone wrong now; I made a mess of that last arrow'. If he had concentrated on the discipline of how to shoot the next arrow properly he might well have come back again on form.

Set yourself an objective – not simply to do as well as you can, for that is too vague, but a specific goal of so many points that it is reasonable to suppose you might with effort achieve. This is especially important in field archery, because if you are in a group containing no other good shots, you have no yardstick against which to measure yourself. You must often create your own incentives. Now, suppose that you are more than half-way through the shoot and realise it is just not possible for you to reach this intended total, then accept the inevitable and switch to an alternative goal, namely, a desired total for each target; if you drop one or two on a target, you can always endeavour to pull back on the next. If you still have no joy, do *not* pack it in and retire, but decide to use the rest of the round as practice, whereupon you will often find that the easing of tension restores the style and the score. The only time I would recommend withdrawing from a shoot is when you are not a member of a nominated team, and when you are physically ill or when the tackle is hopelessly out of order. The act of withdrawing is an admission of defeat that insidiously saps the resistance the next time a similar situation arises.

Examine your motives. What do you shoot for? For fun? Some people do and say it doesn't matter how bad their score is; they just like handling the tackle and being in congenial company. Some are speaking the truth, but I suspect most of making excuses. Most archers would enjoy their archery more if they could score better – yes, score better, not shoot better, as any coach knows. There is a deeper motivation. Ask yourself, why archery? Why not something else? Do I just want to have the exquisite pleasure of shooting the occasional arrow 'straight down the middle', or to win against worthy opposition, or to win anyway, or to go up to get the medal or prize. I mean, what value has it in itself? Is it endeavouring to beat old rivals, or just to measure up to a standard you've set yourself? Do you perhaps wish to please a husband, a wife, a parent or a coach, rather than yourself? Then again, how far do you want to go in archery? What are you prepared to give up to achieve this ambition? Consideration of all these questions will lead to self-knowledge and that is no bad thing.

Improving insight also means gaining in tournament experience. Everyone suffers from nerves if they want to do well at anything – it's an unavoidable feed-back. But there are compensations, for when you find that you can cope with the situation that caused you so many 'butterflies' at the outset, you are able to build on that feeling of confidence. It is a fact that familiarity with a 'stress' situation will make it less fearsome. The anticipation may always be a cause of anxiety and concern, but the actual performance becomes increasingly under control. Remember *you* make the tension; no-one else does. Even if someone is deliberately trying to upset you, you can take confidence in that he probably fears you as a rival, or he wouldn't bother. The only other point to make about 'match nerves' is to be on your guard against the unexpected loss of concentration when you aren't even aware of being under stress. This is especially important on the last few targets which may be critical – yet you know the end is in sight and can get careless.

8

LAYING A COURSE

Whether a course is to be laid and set out for a one or two-day event and then taken down, or whether it is to be permanent, has a bearing on the amount of work involved and the extent to which the natural growth can be modified. Use your judgement in these matters.

SITE

In selecting a site you should consider accessibility, car parking space and security as well as shooting qualities. You would perhaps like to be near a well populated district for the sake of promoting membership, but on the other hand, you have to consider vandalism, only too prevalent today. Field courses, I am afraid, seem to arouse mindless reactions in a certain type of idle layabout with nothing better to do than to attempt to destroy other people's pleasurable activity. So woods with private access are worth considering. Better still are areas which are quite often patrolled by the owners and other responsible people. There may be other discouragements to trespassers, such as clay-pigeon shooting, that take place at times when the archers are not there. If you use grounds where the public are apt to intrude, even illegally, you may have to put up warning signs.

The terrain itself should certainly provide plenty of slope with open, wooded and scrubby areas if possible. It need not be extensive, for with skill and care 14 targets can be set quite safely in 5 or 6 acres (2.5 hect), though more ground is certainly desirable (see Figure 12). Fir plantations are apt to be too gloomy, birch woods are often densely over-grown; beech woods are good with little or no undergrowth; old established

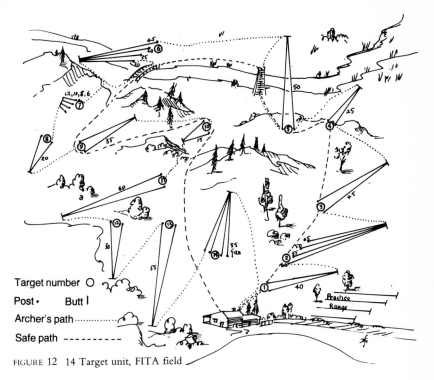

Target number O
Post •   Butt I
Archer's path ··········
Safe path - - - - - - -

FIGURE 12   14 Target unit, FITA field

wide-spread deciduous woodland with oaks and other trees offer
plenty of well-lit and varied shots. Some patches of open ground
are very testing to shoot over, especially where there are areas of
dead ground to confuse the eye. Even well-matured and well-
maintained grounds and lawns are quite possible to use for
temporary set-ups – arrows are less easily lost on turf than in
bracken and leaf-mould, for instance.

Accessibility to the assembly area, toilets and catering facilities
has to be kept in mind, too. Archery is a social pursuit as well as a
sporting activity, so proximity to a country pub is no bad thing.
Provision on the site for a club house and target store is highly
desirable.

THE PRACTICE AREA

Targets must be set up for loosening-up practice, or for checking
equipment, sights and gaps. This area should be safely roped off

or marked off, and provide sufficient target butts for the likely number of archers using the various distances, with clear ground around and behind the butts, and no danger to people or live-stock caused by overshooting the targets by accident. The dis-tances of the targets should be given so as to make the practice more meaningful.

THE COURSE ITSELF

The course must be planned with great care so as, to take into account a number of factors. There should be considerable vari-ety of shots, so that short shots alternate with longer ones; also, some possibility of altering the distance of shots within reason-able limits (particularly important on permanent courses). Abso-lute safety should be maintained so that no arrows are shot in directions that archers or spectators can pass, during shots or in between shots. If a 'safe path' can be arranged for the use of work parties, officials, spectators and archers who finish early or have to leave the course, that is a most valuable facility. It is desirable to damage existing natural growth as little as possible. If you have unrestricted use of a site for a permanent course more 'improvements' can be made, but in general it is better to adapt your plan to the site rather than try to alter the site to fit the plan!

In designing (not actually setting out) the course, an optical range-finder is invaluable. You can look through it, adjust the dials and say, 'Ah, yes, we could get a 55 metre in there.' You cannot use the optical range-finder for setting out the course as it is not sufficiently accurate – a steel tape-measure at least 60 metres long should be used.

In woodland, particular care must be taken to see that the targets are set so as to be visible to short people, and that users of light bows can shoot at them. To check this, take a light bow with you when planning the course, if you have the slightest doubt about overhangs. Remember, too, left-handers need a practical standing position as well as right-handers, tall people as well as short people. Don't forget to leave safe space in front of the posts and overhead for archers using lengthy bows and stabiliser systems. Having designed the courses, a great deal of thought and hard work will be necessary in planning distances, angles, direction arrows, safe walks – even bridges, steps, duck-boards, bow racks, tree shots, and so on, in the case of a permanent course. Directions may be indicated temporarily by coloured tapes tied to trees and twigs as signals for the archers to follow, such as blue course, red course, and so on but it is better to have direction arrows or triangles, which also say what targets can be reached, eg 'to target 12.'

In addition to the target number, it is helpful at the target to be able to distinguish the posts clearly by their colour (junior posts perhaps being set in a different colour) and to see a board or plate which tells how many arrows are allowed from each post and the distances, if it is a marked course.

Finally, when the course is set, targets erected and made secure, one must still check the distances and ensure that the right faces are put on the right butts, and that the correct spare faces are left at the targets when a shoot is in progress. If there is any mistake in face size or distance discovered after archers have begun to shoot through, the error must stay for others to grapple with likewise. This is acutely embarrassing for all concerned, so remember: check and double-check. When all is complete, a plan of the courses can be drawn up, one either posted up in the assembly area, or duplicated and attached to the score boards, so that archers can find their way quickly to the targets on which they start.

9

MAKING AND MENDING

Some archers make and repair their own tackle. Their motives are various and each needs some comment; an archer may choose to make his own equipment for any or all of the following reasons:

1   To save money. This is certainly possible, provided that you make a good job of the article. If, however, you are inexperienced, you may run into expense you had not expected by spoiling costly materials while learning. This would be particularly likely in attempting to make bows without advice. The assembly of arrows from a kit of parts, though, is not going to present any outstanding problems.

2   To get a better match of equipment without going to a lot of expense. For instance the length of arrows could be reduced, the fletchings altered, or a series of strings of different lengths could be made so as to see which suited the bow and arrows best.

3   For the sheer pleasure of craftsmanship and preparing to be a *complete* archer. This is probably the most satisfactory aspect of all. The archer who buys his tackle off the peg, so to speak, can never know the satisfaction enjoyed by the archer who has made his own bow, assembled his own arrows, made an ideal bowstring and boasts a handsomely tooled leather quiver.

The tools needed are those acquired by any handyman, such as fine-tooth saws and hack-saws, hand drills, pliers, chisels, and files of various grades and shapes. A work bench and vice are particularly valuable. More sophisticated tools than these can be very useful, but they are not essential. Some specialised equipment such as string jigs and fletching jigs will be needed, but even these are not difficult to make. As regards skill, provided that you know how to use the tools themselves, the processes are quite easily learnt, requiring care and patience rather than dexterity. With materials, you will be well advised to deal only with specialist archery suppliers, as they alone are likely to have the required specifications. They are also very willing to give valuable advice to the archer craftsman, or put him in touch with experts.

WOODEN ARROWS

Archers in the Traditional and Hunting style classes will want to make wooden arrows. The best, indeed the only worthwhile, material is Port Orford cedar 32″ (81 cm) long available in two standard dimensions: $5/16″$ and $11/32″$. The former will be suitable for arrows of 26″ (66 cm) or less in bows of 40 lbs (18 kg) or less at 26″ draw. If arrows are 27″ (69 cm) or longer, and the bow 40 lbs or more at 28″ (71 cm), then the stouter $11/32″$ arrow stave is required.

The best available matching is essential, so that all staves are of the same diameter, spine, grain and weight. To get a satisfactory matched set of eight, you may have to purchase three times as many and regrade them. If you can sort through a large number so much the better, but the supplier will not be too keen on having the quality of his sample reduced by having the best staves taken out. Because of the natural characteristics of wood, staves may match for spine and not for weight, and vice versa, so extra care in selection is required. Of course, one may retain the spine and reduce weight by slightly barrelling the heavier staves, that is, by removing material at the extremities by tapering slightly and leaving the middle alone, but this entails more trouble than most people are prepared to go to.

Having selected, say, a dozen staves that are of a spine suitable to your arrow length and bow-weight, check for straightness. You can straighten a slight bend by steam heat, but there is the chance the bend may return later, so it is better to start with straight shafts. Now you can proceed to attach the piles. If these are over-size, they will slip on without obliging you to reduce the size of the shaft. If you wish to have flush-fitting piles, you will need to purchase a shaft-cutter or do some neat work with a knife and a file. Oversize piles are easier to put on straight and are stronger at the junction with the wood. They are perhaps more liable to pull off in the target, but in any case I would recommend riveting on any piles to wooden arrows with brass wire inserted through a small diameter drill hole and filed flush, even after the piles have been secured with ferrule cement or other glue. Riveted piles will not come off even in stramit butts. Crimping is another way of securing, with a special tool or with a centre punch, but this spoils the appearance of the pile and is not very successful in making a secure job.

Next, measure for length and cut off the surplus. Now to attach the nocks. Here it is important to ensure that the cock-feather will lie on the edge of the grain of the wood, since the shaft is stronger that way. This means that the slot of the nock must be at right-angles to the grain, as shown in Figure 13, and that the index nib of an index nock is aligned with the edge of the grain. If the nock has an internal taper, use a tapering tool (there is one provided on shaft-cutters as a rule). Be careful not to remove too much wood or you will shorten the arrow. Also, take the utmost care to ensure that the taper is central. If it is lop-sided, the nock will not sit on straight and will break off under the impact of the string after a few looses.

Choose the right size of nock for the shaft and for the string. Care has to be taken to ensure that all arrows end up the same length. You could, of course, fit the nocks before you cut down the staves and take care to fit the piles accurately for length. With some types of pile, this could be easier. In gluing the nock with water-proof glue, put some of the glue inside the nock as well as on the shaft, and twist it on to get a good adhesion, adjust for angle to the grain, and wipe off excess glue. At this stage you should seal and polish or paint the shafts, for they must be waterproof, as much to keep *in* a desirable amount of humidity as to keep *out* excess damp – a dried-out shaft is a brittle shaft. Again, the amount of humidity in a shaft can make a lot of difference to its weight and spine characteristics, so you need to stabilise the water content by sealing.

Now to attach the fletching. Have regard to the size and length of shaft in selecting fletching, which should be 4″ (100 mm) or 5″ (130 mm) long. Colour, as we said before, is important, for you need to be able to see the arrows in the target. If you buy prepared fletchings from a supplier they will be from the same side of the bird. If mixed left and right wing feathers were used they would set up contrary pressures so that the arrow could not fly true. A left wing fletching cannot be made to match a right wing fletching for the underside and topside of the feathers are opposed. Check that the fletchings are of similar thickness and quality, too.

Clean away the polish or paint in the exact places where the fletchings will lie. Use a waterproof glue and do not use an excessive amount, because it is no stronger than a sufficient application and looks unsightly. It is possible with skill to attach fletchings by hand and eye using thread to hold them straight while the glue is drying, in which case the thread is removed after the glue has set, but you are strongly advised to use a fletching jig designed for the size of fletching you are using. This will be much more exact, and exactness is essential in fletching. Leave a space of about 1¼″ (32 mm) between the slot of the nock and the back end of the fletchings and see that all three fletchings are in line. Impact adhesives might seem to offer a speedy way of securing fletchings but they do not dry out sufficiently to make a secure attachment that will last.

Feather fletching can be put on straight, that is, parallel to the shaft, and the arrow will still rotate in flight, owing to the differing air-flow over the rough and smooth surfaces of the feathers and to the actual innate construction of the feather itself which resists pressure from the underside and yields to it from the topside. This rotation is desirable and gives the same effect as rifling in a gun. In view of the relatively large size of the fletchings you do not really need to increase the spinning action of the fletchings, but you can do so if you wish at the expense of losing some arrow speed, by off-setting the feathers, that is, setting them at a slight angle, say 2°, to the shaft. If you do this, you must make sure that the underside of the feathers faces the pile of the arrow and meets the air-flow; otherwise you will be defeating your object (see Figure 13). Roughly number the arrows in pencil. Next shoot them at a distance at which you can be fairly confident of uniformity in your own shooting and plot their behaviour. Shoot them in random order, so as to avoid building in any doubts you may have over individual arrows. Then group match the best of the arrows. There are so many variables in using natural materials that it is not usually possible to ensure a high degree of uniformity without a practical test. Renumber the arrows according to your findings and finish by cresting and naming or initialling them, and pack them in such a way as to prevent the fletchings being compressed or otherwise damaged.

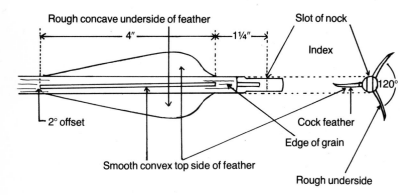

FIGURE 13 Fletching wooden arrows

Repairs will be needed occasionally. If one fletching needs attention, take the utmost care to match for wing side, shape, quality, and, to a lesser extent, for colour. Set the angle scrupulously to match that of the fletchings that remain and clean away all traces of old glue. If the nock needs replacing, and cannot easily be levered off with the thumbs, you will find that attempts to cut it off will lead to cutting away some of the wood as well, so it is better to set fire to the nock and remove the remnants with a pair of pliers when it is soft. In doing this, be careful to hold the arrow fairly upright, so as not to set fire to the fletchings, yet not so vertical that hot melted plastic runs down on to the shaft or your hands. Blow the flame out before it begins to char the wood and clean up the taper before affixing the replacement nock exactly in its correct position relative to the cock-feather.

Should the piles of several arrows get broken off, it is possible to restore them to use by re-footing them. This means putting on a hardwood two–point splice about 6½" (165 mm) long. There should be at least 2" (50 mm) of solid hardwood at the pile end. Cut off the original shaft, say, 1½" short of the junction with the old pile, and plane the last 4½" (115 mm) to a flat tapered chisel edge *with* the grain, but with the edge left as thick as the kerf of the tenon-saw that you are going to use to cut a slot in the 7½" (190 mm) piece of hardwood that will form the footing. It should be the same diameter as the arrow shaft, but square in cross-section. Cut a slot 4½" (115 mm) deep lengthwise also *with* the grain so that it won't split when you insert the tapered wedge of the main shaft (Figure 14). Bind the uncut end section of the hardwood or place it in a clamp. Apply glue to the surfaces and insert the wedge, lashing or clamping to keep it in place while the glue dries. Make sure that the alignment of footing and original shaft is perfect. When the glue has set, carefully plane off the

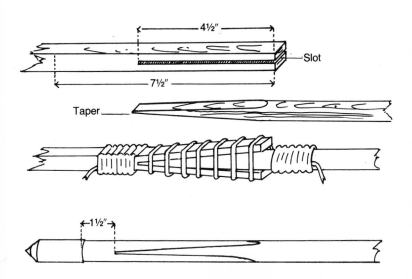

FIGURE 14   Splicing a footing

'ears' of the footing, round off the irregularities and finish with a file, dowel-plate and glass-paper. Cut to length and fit pile.

An arrow reinforced with a footing like this will weigh more than a 'self' arrow, that is to say, an arrow made of one piece of wood throughout, and it will have a more forward point of balance, but that is not necessarily a bad thing. There is no reason why one should not foot arrows in the first place, although it obviously takes longer, and wooden field arrows are liable to be lost or broken in mid-shaft, so they are considered more expendable than alloy. Professionally footed arrows usually have three or four-point splices created by means of a special tool.

ALLOY ARROWS

Many of the processes involved in making alloy arrows are identical to those employed in making wooden arrows. With alloy arrows it is a matter of assembling the pieces that are provided, which proves cheaper than buying already assembled arrows (where you will be paying for the craftsmanship of the fletching). The shafts may be bought cut to the length you require and ready nocked and piled, or you can get them 32" (81 cm) long, the nock end swaged, and the nocks and piles loose.

Fit the nock, gluing it so that the cock-feather position can be on the side of the shaft that bears the trade mark and specification, since you won't want to wear that away while repeatedly loading and shooting the bow. Allowing for the length of the projecting part of the pile, cut for length. If you have access to a metal tube cutter, that's fine; if not, use a fine hacksaw, being very careful to cut at right-angles to the shaft or you will have an unsightly gap left between pile-tip and shaft-end. You could trim it up with a file, but then you'd lose length. If you can conveniently get the shaft cut professionally, do so, but you may need a shaft cut to an odd draw-length, and need to phone through the instructions which could be difficult to get exact. Length of arrows, especially with users of clickers, is so critical that you cannot be too careful in this respect. Remove any burr that may have formed on the tube where it has been cut and offer up the piles for fit. They should just fit into the shaft, but be removable without undue force.

Use a hot-melt mixture of resin and beeswax, as this will give good adhesion and yet allow you to remove piles at any time for replacement by the application of heat so low that it cannot harm the alloy tube. Should you fix piles in with metal-fixing compounds they will stay in all right, but they will be impossible to remove. When you have warmed the end of the tube and the pile and applied the hot-melt from the stick to the pile, put them firmly together and hold a moment under cold water, or you may find that the air pressure inside the tube can cause the pile to slide away a few millimetres, or even come off, while it is still warm. Clean off the excess glue.

Fletching is done in a jig in the same way as for wooden arrows, but a smaller size of jig would be suitable since the fletchings need not be so large. See that the collet or nock-locator is the right size to accept the nock size you are using. If it is too small, you may scar the nock and the fletchings may be set too near the nock. If it is too big, the arrow will be free to move, causing undesirable variation in fletching angles. You can have locators for four-fletch angles, but in field archery, three-fletch is almost universal. You will very likely be using plastic vanes, either slotted, rigid or flexible. In this case there is more point in off-setting the fletching than when using feathers, because an arrow straight-fletched with plastic vanes will not rotate. It is a controversial point whether to have the arrow rotate or not, but most archers prefer that it should. Even so, don't offset more than 2°, or you will set up needless drag and consequent loss of velocity.

Off-setting with feather fletching has to match the left or right wing character of the feather. Off-setting with plastic vanes can be set so as to cause either clockwise or anti-clockwise rotation according to the direction of the off-set. You may wonder if being right-handed or left-handed makes any difference to which rotation you employ? I don't see how it can, because the arrow cannot rotate while it is still on the string, and it can hardly rotate much, if at all, before it passes the bow. It should not touch the bow anyway, once it has parted company with the string. Some archers have more trouble than others in getting fletchings to stay firmly stuck to the shafts. It may be that they are less careful in preparing the surface. Absolute cleanliness is essential. All traces of grease must certainly be removed by alcohol or other solvents. An application of lacquer may assist the gluing process. Lastly, you should make sure that there are no gaps or air-spaces where damp could get in under the vane. The rigid vanes are particularly vulnerable, because they can be nearly detached before the archer is aware that anything is wrong with them at all. When you set the shaft in the jig remember to set the cock-vane on the side of the shaft that bears the specification engraved on it. To remove damaged nocks from alloy arrows you can quite easily cut them off if they are external fitting, or unscrew them if they are internal. If an internal fitting nock is broken off, you may have to insert a hot nail held in pliers to soften the plastic before you can remove it.

Under maintenance of alloy arrows comes the question of straightening. A very large bend can easily be seen by looking along the shaft as it is rotated. A very small bend can be detected by spinning the shaft against the support of another arrow, when the bent arrow will chatter. Precise location of the bend can only be achieved by using an arrow straightener with a micrometer dial attached. Straightening can be done by controlled application of force from a lever after rotating the shaft to give the greatest plus reading on the dial. Thereafter, the whole shaft should be trued up, until the least possible movement of the dial hand occurs wherever the arrow shaft is rotated throughout its whole length. Straightening by hand is not going to be anything but rough and ready. Straightening pliers are a little better, for one can set a stop-screw to control the amount of force applied, and one can feel the stiffness caused by the high point of a bend if the handles of the pliers are held lightly closed against the resistance of the shaft. But for accuracy, a micrometer dial is needed.

Anodising of shafts resists corrosion, but all arrows, whether anodised or not, should be thoroughly dried before being put away, if they have been used in the wet. Look for cracks in the shaft. If they should appear, discard the shaft. The irregularity will show up on a micrometer straightening aid.

BOWSTRINGS

Any archer worth his salt has at least two strings to his bow. You are advised to make them yourself as in this way you can have them exactly the length that you have found to be ideal when tuning the bow. By marking the jig you can be sure of turning out others that are identical.

Materials

A great variety of materials has been used throughout the ages. Linen and hemp are still in use today, but only for the traditional strings of the traditional longbow. Linen is a good string material, but very variable in quality. If it is kept moderately humid it stays strong; if it is allowed to dry out it becomes useless and brittle, so it must be kept well waxed. But, as I said, it is only used by longbow purists. Good material can be obtained unpolished in small 'cops' from shoemakers.

For all other bows only two basic materials are in use, Dacron and the non-stretch fibres. In addition, for serving purposes, monofilament, soft-twist nylon and braided nylon are available. All these are man-made materials and are therefore fairly uniform in production and quality. Dacron B50 has a breaking limit of 50 lbs (23 kg) per strand, hence its code-name. It is a little stretchy, especially before being shot in, so that it may be necessary to allow for this in manufacture. Because of the slight elasticity of the string, the bracing height will need to be a little higher than with non-stretch fibres, for the arrow will be delivered slightly in front of the bracing height. Dacron strings are very durable and impervious to moisture so they will only need waxing to keep the strands conveniently together, if at all.

Non-stretch carbon fibres (more correctly, carbonised fibres) really do not stretch noticeably in use at all, not even when an arrow is loosed. So the string will be made initially longer than one of Dacron (say, ¾″), for it will not extend when the bow is braced. Also, since the arrow will be delivered at bracing height, the bracing-height may be set a little lower than with Dacron. A new string made of non-stretch fibres should be made the same length as an old one. Ideally, of course, you should make several at the same time, but not so many as to run the risk of deterioration while being stored. Carbon fibre is strongest longitudinally and weakened if it is sharply angled, or the fibres crushed, so it is not advisable to use monofilament serving, metal nock locks, or even angled nock-slots. A well-made non-stretch string will last up to 3,000 shots depending very much on the technique of the archer and the care and attention he gives to his equipment. However, if a replacement string is needed in the middle of a tournament, the archer can put on a new string and shoot with every expectation of an identical performance. As it is inadvisable to let a string actually break on the bow, some archers include, say, 4 strands of Dacron in with the requisite number of non-stretch fibre strands (from 14 to 18, for they are a little thinner than Dacron). These do no work in normal shooting and admittedly add weight, but should the string break, they will hold on and let the bow down lightly. If black Dacron is used together with black carbon fibres, the two will blend together indistinguishably.

Monofilament gives a very fast loose and is often used for the centre-serving of Dacron strings. It does need careful application for a firm fit that will not come loose at the ends, or the whole serving will unwind in an instant. Since it is available in various gauges, it is possible by reference to the charts of suppliers to ensure a neat nock fit in accordance with the number of strands used in the main body of your strings and your choice of nock make and size. The soft-twist nylon or the braided nylon is used for the loops of strings made of both string materials, the braided being particularly suitable for the centre-serving of non-stretch fibre strings.

Serving

Before you make a string you will need to practise making a whipping or serving, and especially practise finishing it off. Whether you serve by hand off the reel or use a serving tool, remember that if you are serving from left to right, the spool should go away from you over the string; while if you are serving from right to left, it should come towards you over the

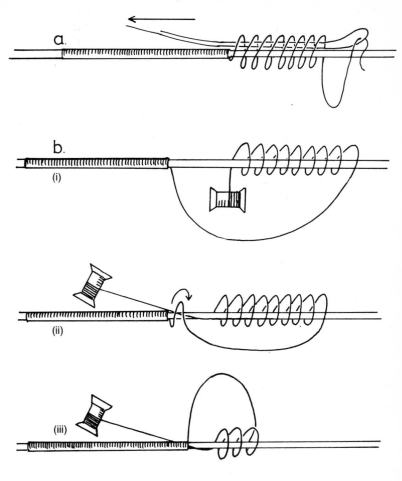

FIGURE 15 Finishing a serving

string. To start, insert the end of the serving thread through the string and firmly wind over it at least 8 turns of the thread. That takes care of that end. Continue working until you reach the other end of the area to be served, being careful to keep the turns laid with an even tension neatly against each other and not cross-threaded. Now comes the tricky part – at least, it's tricky to explain, but not so difficult to do. The diagrams may help.

You can use an extra loop of separate thread to pull back the free end under the last 8 turns as in Figure 15 (a). Leave enough slack at the end of the serving to allow you to pull it under the firm serving. Alternatively, you can follow the instructions in Figure 15 (b). This is strongly recommended because you do not need to cut the thread from the reel or spool, which is a great advantage in making an 'endless' string as you will see later. One thing to watch, though, is to see that the loop left at the end does not tangle upon itself as you pull it through. Ease it through gradually, keeping the loop open with a pencil as you gently pull on the free end until it is all through.

THE LAID-IN BOWSTRING

The method described is the traditional one, for longbow purists. It is intended for linen or hemp, but you can use Dacron B, if you wish. If you are using linen, find the breaking strain of one strand. It may very likely be 7 lbs (3 kg), for the thread is thin. If it is Dacron B50 you are using then it will be 50 lbs (23 kg). Divide 6 times the bow-weight by the breaking strain of linen to find out how many strands to use. Divide 12 times the bow-weight by the breaking strain of Dacron to find out how many Dacron strands to use. The reason for the factor of 12 is to make sure you get a string that is not so thin as to be painful to use, unstable in action, and troublesome to fit for nocks.

Whichever material you are using, round up the figures to an even number. One more thing to do: have prepared some softened beeswax if you are to use dry linen or hemp. If you are to use waxed Dacron, there is no need to use anything else. To soften wax until it is the consistency of processed cheese, cut it into small pieces and put it into a small screw-top jar together with a teaspoonful of real turpentine (white spirit will work, but not so well). After a few days the pieces of wax will be soft and pliable, like putty. You use this to work into the string while you are twisting and making it, so don't get it too soft or it will be too slippery to handle.

The Method

Calculate or observe the length of string required between the nocks of a braced bow. Add on 20″ (50 cm). This allows for the timber hitch at one end, and the turning of the loop at the other. Put in two nails in a plank or bench the total distance apart. Screw a cup-hook into a wall or other support at waist height, leaving yourself room to retire at least 6' (2 m) from it. You will need this space to tense the string while you are making it. Wind off the requisite number of strands round the two nails, so that between the nails are the numbers of strands you want in the main body of the string. Cut right through the strands by one of the nails (the one where you started) and hang the middle of the opposite end (where the other nail was) over the cup hook. Pull all strands even. You will then have half the strands in one hand and half of them in the other. Tug at the individual strands a little in order to make the ends slightly irregular so that later they may be lost in the body of the string.

Laying up the String

Wax the last 12" (30 cm) or so, if the material is not already waxed. Hold the two bundles about 9" (23 cm) from the cut ends between the fore-finger and thumb of the left hand and pull firmly against the resistance of the hook. Taking one bundle at a time between the fore-finger and thumb of the right hand, roll and twist the threads to the right (clockwise) and lay the bundles over each other to the left (anti-clockwise) as in Figure 16 (a). Form a piece of twisted string in this way long enough to form the circumference of the loop you require, say, 2½" (50 mm).

Making the Loop

Then cast off your threads from the hook and put the piece you have been working on over the hook instead. Marry each bundle of free ends with the opposite piece of main string as in Figure 16 (b) and carry on twisting the married bundles as before to the right and laying to the left until you have lost the ends. You will then have formed a loop as in Figure 16 (c) that will never come unravelled *provided* it is kept twisted up in the same direction as it was made.

Making the Tail

Carefully pay out the threads to the other end. Cut through and

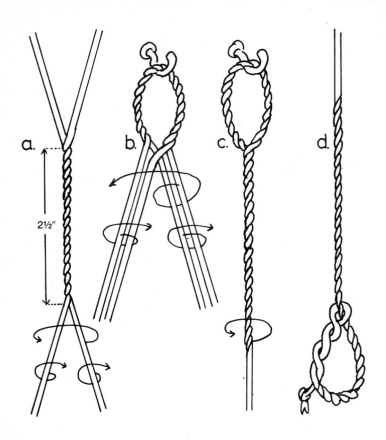

FIGURE 16   The laid-in string

arrange them straight and parallel. At a suitable point from the
end, say 12″ (30 cm) begin making a straight piece of twisted
string as you did at first, and carry right on down to the end
where you tie an over-hand knot. Wax the whole string and twist
it to the left (anti-clockwise) so as to tighten up the made string
and put about one turn per inch all the way through. Polish the
string with the hand or with a piece of paper or leather held in the
hand to warm the wax and bond the string together a little. Tie a
timber hitch in the loopless end and adjust it until the bow is
braced to your satisfaction (Figure 16 (d)).

The Centre-serving

Allow 3" (80 mm) above the centre of the bow and 5" (130 mm) under it normally, but you may have to consider regulations of the association you belong to that refer to the position of the top end of the serving. Start serving at the bottom and work towards the top while the string is on the braced bow and held conveniently taut. If you find nylon thread abhorrent as being untraditional, use carpet thread instead. Finish off the serving by one of the methods already described.

Remember, this string will not slip or come apart unless you tie an incorrect timber hitch in the end, or attempt to twist the string in the opposite direction to that in which it was made. By the way, the direction of twist in the manufacture of the original thread dictates the subsequent twists you may put into it, so it is not possible to make this string in any other direction than that described above. Left-handers please note. With experience you can make this string very quickly indeed, and introduce refinements, like reinforcing strands in the loop and tail, and laying in with three tails at the loop.

THE 'ENDLESS' STRING

Before you can make a string you will need a jig, as shown in Figure 17. The swivel arms at the ends enable the four posts, round which the string material is wound, to be set square to allow you to serve the loop ends, or to be set in line to allow you to close the loops. The centre slide enables you to adjust for any length of string you are likely to require.

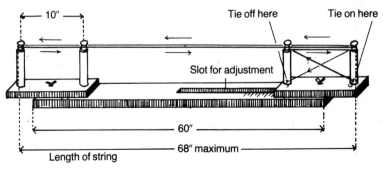

FIGURE 17 String jig

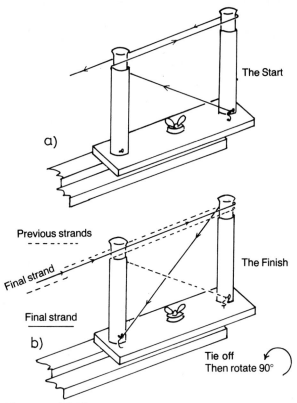

The Start

a)

Previous strands

Final strand

The Finish

Final strand

b)

Tie off
Then rotate 90°

FIGURE 18   The start and finish

Decide how many strands you need, either by using the formula already mentioned for Dacron, or by referring to the manufacturers' recommendations, or by seeing how many you had in the previous string. Remember, a thick string reduces cast but is stable; a thin string gives added speed but is apt to be over elastic and create other problems. A 12 strand string is fairly standard for men's bows. It is nearly as important for a string to be of a convenient thickness as to be strong enough.

The Method

Set up the jig with the posts in line. If you have a used Dacron string of the right length, take out any twists you may have in it, and loop it over the outside posts and pull taut. Tighten up the

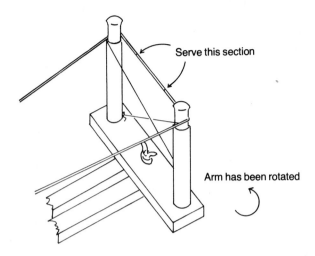

Serve this section

Arm has been rotated

FIGURE 19   Serving the loop

wing nuts on the slide and remove the string. Now the tension is off, slacken the nuts and move the slide to bring the posts ⅛th of an inch closer (3 mm) so that a slightly shorter string will be made. This will allow for the initial stretch of the new string. Mark where you set the slide for future reference.

Put a short rod through the spool of Dacron, so that you can reel off the thread without twisting it in the process. Tie off one end on the nail provided, take the thread 6 times down the length of the posts, having first gone across the short distance between the first two posts (see Figures 17 and 18 (a)), and 6 times back, as that will put 12 strands along the middle of the string. Then tie off the Dacron on the other nail as shown in Figure 18 (b) and cut off the surplus. At the end of the jig where the ends have been tied off, mark the extremities of the bottom loop in pencil (or chalk, if it is black Dacron you are using). Turn the swivel arms to right angles so that you can serve the space between your two marks with soft-twist nylon either from the reel or from a string-server as shown in Figure 19. Serve from left to right, taking the spool over away from you.

When you reach the end of the space to be served, do *not* cut the thread, but finish as shown in Figure 15 (b) (iii) on page 135, leaving the spool attached. Turn the pillars into line again and undo the ends of the thread where they are attached to the nails. Match up the ends of the serving at the point where the loop will be closed. Wind the end threads along the standing part of the string (see Figure 20) and serve firmly down over them for about 5″ or 6″ (120-150 mm) making sure that you continue the movement of the spool in the same direction as before, namely, over away from you if you are working from left to right, or over towards you if you are now working from right to left. Get a firm whipping at the point where the loop closes. This loop only needs to be big enough to go over the nock at the bottom end of the bow with a little to spare. A dab of impact adhesive will help to secure the end of the serving without damaging the string fibres as hard drying glues may do.

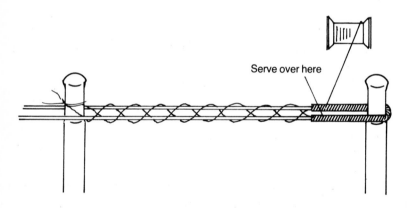

Serve over here

FIGURE 20   Closing the loop

Now measure the depth of loop required at the other end of the string. This will be the top end, so make sure the loop is going to be large enough to slide down the top limb of the bow before it is braced. Proceed in the same manner as for the other loop. When you have finished both loops, take the string off one pillar and put in a few twists (either way with an 'endless' string) to encourage the strands to stay together and equalise tension (which should be perfect anyway if you have been careful). Rub the string lightly to bond the threads if you are using waxed Dacron.

String the bow with it and brace it and draw the bow a few times (without loosing it, of course) to stretch the string. Check to see that the length is approximately right. If it is braced too low, you can brace it higher by up to half an inch by twisting the string, but there is a limit to the amount of twist it is advisable to put into a string. 1½ turns per inch is the absolute limit and is really too much for a satisfactory performance. If it is too short there is nothing you can do about it and you will have to make another. But provided that it is all right, mark where the centre-serving is to be and serve with monofilament, or nylon thread. If you shoot barebow in GNAS and FITA, you may find it necessary to serve up beyond the eye-brow at your standard anchor point. If you shoot freestyle, the serving must not extend above the point of your nose.

Using Non-stretch Fibres

There will be no difference in basic method. You will have to remember several points, though:

1   The string will need to be a little longer than a Dacron string, because it will not stretch at all when the bow is braced.
2   There must be no knot tied in it; we have avoided tying one in the Dacron method, because a knot is a source of weakness. If you don't believe it, tie a firm knot in a loop of bowstring material and break it between two cylindrical toggles and see where it breaks! A knot is particularly to be avoided in using the non-stretch fibres.
3   You will have to use rather more threads to get the same thickness of string.
4   You may wish to include a few strands of Dacron as a security measure against sudden breakage.
5   You don't want to have to twist these non-stretch fibres much – they function best when nearly straight.
6   On no account should you centre-serve non-stretch fibres with monofilament, but you should use braided nylon instead.

Maintenance

One is not likely to wish to repair a bow-string, except for re-serving perhaps, if serving has come adrift, but the strings should be kept carefully. Linen strings should be kept moist coiled in a tin, and well waxed. Dacron strings are sometimes strung on hooks in the lid of a tackle box, and it probably does them no harm, but they would be better kept coiled in a grease-proof packet. Non-stretch strings must *not* be strung on hooks, but must be coiled without any kinks in a separate packet for each.

Nocking Points and Kissers

If nock sets are used on Dacron strings they must not be set so close together as to pinch the arrow nock at full draw. Locate the nocking point by using a square and testing at short range as in the first bow-tuning exercise. If you are using non-stretch fibres, then use waxed dental floss to build a rib above and below the nocking point by making two separate servings. If you wish to thicken the string at this point to hold on the nocks that would otherwise be too loose a fit, then you can use dental floss for this purpose, too. If you decide to add a dab of glue to hold all firm, then use an impact adhesive first so as not to risk damage to fibres from harder-drying glues.

The same procedure can be applied to the kisser, if you use one, for it must be prevented from moving or rattling. Serve a short length of dental floss above and below the kisser and fix with impact glue before adding any harder glue, like fletching cement.

TARGETS

Butts may be made, as mentioned in Chapter 2, of about 16 to 20 thicknesses of flattened corrugated cardboard packing cases lashed together with string. Extra stopping power is provided by incorporating several sheets of polythene or plastic between some of the panels. All rivets and staples must be removed before assembly.

I would not consider earth or turf butts because it is virtually impossible to ensure that no stones are present to damage the arrows. Wood-wool in tightly strapped bundles cut so that a cross-cut section provides a flat surface on which to put the target faces, is practicable only for permanent butts, because it is so thick and heavy. Another useful material is celotex, or insulating board, cut into 5" wide strips. These are laid in a stack clamped between uprights so that the archer shoots his arrows into the edge of the material. It is necessary to soak the celotex in oil so as to render it waterproof and to strengthen it. If removable nuts are used on the vertical frame supports, it is possible to undo these, remove badly shot-up central strips, and move into their place sound strips of celotex. When soaked in oil, these butts are quite heavy, but eminently suitable for permanent butts.

OTHER ITEMS

The making of leather bracers, tabs and quivers is a job that will appeal to the archer who has skill in that direction and the necessary tools, but will not be dealt with here.

It would also be impracticable to deal with bow-making in this book – the subject would require a book to itself to deal fully with only a few designs and methods. Unless you are able to work very accurately with tools, make up the jigs and formers required, and have exact directions to follow, you could end up by wasting expensive materials and suffering severe disappointment after expending a lot of effort and time. It is a fact, though, that a few archers do make very efficient and handsome bows, and it is certainly a great satisfaction to have made one's own bow and shoot in it.

Whether you make up your own equipment or use the best that professionals can supply, I hope that this survey of field archery will have stimulated you to join with me in the fascination of field. Good shooting!

GLOSSARY

ANCHOR To set the hand firmly against some part of the face.

ANCHOR-POINT The location chosen for the anchor.

ANCHOR-TAB Finger-protection incorporating a 'shelf' to locate under the jaw.

ARROW-PLATE Adjustable plate to move arrow-rest out or in.

ARROW-REST Projection from bow for supporting arrow while being drawn and aimed.

BACK (of bow) Side of the bow furthest from the string.

BELLY (of bow) Side of bow nearest the string, also called the face.

BLUNT Flattened arrow-head, useful for stunning small game.

BOLT Arrow for cross-bow.

BOSS Round target, usually made of compressed straw, or similar material.

BOW QUIVER Attachment to bow to hold arrows as for hunting.

BRACE To set the bow string loops in the bow-nocks ready for shooting.

BRACER Arm guard.

BRACING-HEIGHT The distance between the bow and the string when braced, variously measured.

BROADHEAD Sharp steel arrow-head for killing game.

BRUSH BUTTON Device attached to string to prevent twigs, etc, lodging in end of bow while being carried braced.

BULLET PILES Arrow-points with bullet-shaped heads.

BUSHING   Threaded inserts to allow stabiliser rods to be attached to a bow.

BUTT   Arrow-stop in field archery on which faces are placed.

CANT   To tilt the bow from the vertical.

CAST   The velocity with which the bow delivers the arrow.

CENTRE-SERVING   The material wound round the middle section of the string to reduce wear.

CLICKER   Audible draw-check.

CLOSING TOOL   Pliers designed to secure nock-sets to bow-string.

COCK FEATHER   In three-fletched arrows, the fletching which is set at right angles to the nock.

COMPENSATORS   See TFC's

COMPOSITE   A bow made of more than one basic limb material.

COMPOUND   A bow which provides a mechanical advantage by pulleys or the like.

CONICAL PILES   Arrow points with a straight taper.

CREEP   To fail to maintain draw-length before the loose.

CRESTING   Coloured bands on arrow shaft for decoration and/or identification.

DACRON   Man made fibre for bowstrings.

DAMPERS   See TFC's.

DEAD LOOSE   A releasing of the string without recoil of the loosing hand.

DRAW   To bend the bow by pulling the string.

DRAW-CHECK   Indicator that arrow is full drawn – can be audible or visual.

DRAW-LENGTH   The distance an archer can draw the string; also the distance a bow may be safely drawn to, or measured to.

DRAW-WEIGHT   The poundage required to draw the bow a given distance.

EXTENSION-SIGHT   Bow-sight on a projecting arm to increase eye-to-sight distance for greater accuracy of aim.

FACE   The side of the bow facing the archer.

FACES (Field)   The scoring targets in field archery.

FINGER-TAB   Finger protection on the string hand.

FLETCH   To attach feathers or vanes to an arrow shaft.

FLETCHINGS   Either feathers or plastic vanes to keep arrow on course.

FLETCHING-JIG   Clamp to set accurate angle of fletching to shaft while gluing.

FLIPPER-REST   L-shaped arrow rest that moves aside as arrow passes.

FLOU-FLOU (or FROU-FROU) Arrow with massive spiral feather fletching to slow it rapidly in flight.

FOLLOW THROUGH   Movement of both hands apart on loose.

FOOTING   Spliced reinforcement at pile end of wooden arrow.

FULL-DRAW   Position where archer has drawn the arrow to his full length, and string hand is at anchor-point.

FUR FLETCH   Coloured rabbit fur attached to arrow behind fletching to create 'bomb-burst' effect on impact, so it may be seen more easily.

GAP   Vertical distance observed between arrow-point and target.

GAPPING or GAP-SHOOTING   Using a system in barebow of calculating the gaps required at various distances.

GROUP   A close pattern of arrows in the target.

HEEL   To apply pressure too low on the handle.

HELICAL FLETCH   Fletchings put on in a true spiral as distinct from off-set or angled fletching.

HOT-MELT   Mixture of beeswax and resin, suitable for securing piles to arrow shafts, yet permitting them to be removed when heated.

INSTINCTIVE   Method of shooting without deliberate aiming; often incorrectly applied to any method not employing sights.

KISSER   Small button attached to the string as lip or nose mark.

LAMINATIONS   Flat strips of material, from which bow limbs and handles may be built up.

LEVEL   A spirit-level to ensure that the bow is being held vertically.

LIMB   The working part of a bow, upper or lower. May be detachable.

LONGBOW   Properly speaking, a bow of traditional design with stirrup-shaped cross-section.

MONOFILAMENT   Non-stranded bow serving material similar to fishing line.

NOCK   To put an arrow on the string; also attachment to arrow to enable it to fit onto the string.

NOCK-LOCKS   Buttons to provide positive nocking guides for arrows.

NOCKING-POINT   The chosen position where the arrow fits onto the string.

NOCK-SETS   Thin metal bands protected by softer material to provide clip-on nocking guides for arrows.

OFFSET FLETCHING   Fletchings put on at an angle to make arrow spin.

PEEP-SIGHT   A sight on the bow-string.

PILE   The sharp point of a competition arrow (not a broad-head)

PILE CEMENT   'Glue' for securing arrow-points.

PLASTIC VANES   Fletchings made of plastic.

PLUNGER-BUTTON   Spring-loaded button to absorb shock of arrow when leaving bow, making matching less critical.

POINT OF AIM   Pre-selected mark on which to aim arrow-pile in order to hit target.

PORVAIR   Water-resistant man-made material used for tabs.

PRESSURE-POINT   Vertical part of the arrow-rest which the arrow actually contacts. Can be cushioned or spring-loaded.

QUIVER   Arrow-holder worn on the person.

RECURVE   Tips of the bow limb that curve away from the archer also a bow incorporating this design.

RELEASE or RELEASE-AID   Device to facilitate sharper loose.

RISER   Handle section of bow to which limbs are attached.

ROUND   Set number of arrows shot in a competition, or set number of targets.

SERVING   Binding of material on the string at loops or centre.

SHAFT   Main part of arrow, excluding fletchings, nock and pile.

SIGHT BAR or SIGHT TRACK   Bar on which sight block moves.

SIGHT PIN   Projection which is aligned with the mark aimed at.

SIGHT WINDOW   Cut-away part of a centre-shot bow riser.

SLING   Device to retain bow in archer's hand when shot with an open hand.

SOFT-TWIST NYLON   Multi-filament thread for serving.

SPINE   Measure of stiffness of an arrow shaft or stave.

SPRINGY   Coiled spring to serve as a cushioned arrow-rest.

STABILISER   Any weight or rod attached to or incorporated in a bow to reduce torque.

STACK   Excessive increase in draw-weight on approaching full draw length.

STAVE   The dowel rod from which a wooden arrow is made.

STRING KEEPER   Device to secure string to bow when unbraced.

TAKE-DOWN   A bow with readily detachable limbs.

TILLER   To shape bow limbs for true balance.

TORQUE   Rotary movement of bow in the hand on loose, both vertical and horizontal.

TFC's   Torque Flight Compensators. Flexible bushings to damp down the shock effect of stabilisers.

TUNE   To adjust shooting tackle to produce optimum performance.

VANE   Plastic fletching.

V-BAR   Attachment to bow to allow fitting of two or more stabilisers from one socket.

INDEX